for a time like this

E. H. JOHNSON

for a time like this

STUDIES FOR
SALVATION TODAY
AND MISSION TODAY

FRIENDSHIP PRESS
NEW YORK

Library of Congress Cataloging in Publication Data

Johnson, Edward H.
For a time like this.

Includes bibliographical references.
1. Salvation. 2. Missions. I. Title.
BT751.2.J63 234 73-3087
ISBN 0-377-03001-5

acknowledgements

The following credits express our appreciation to the publishers and writers who have allowed us to use their materials in this book.

All Bible quotations in this book are reprinted from *The New English Bible,* copyright 1961 and 1970 by Oxford and Cambridge University Presses.

Page 24, From *Waiting for Godot* by Samuel Beckett. Reprinted by permission of Grove Press, Inc. Copyright © 1954 by Grove Press, Inc.

Page 25, From "Help!" by Lennon-McCartney. Copyright © 1965 Northern Songs Ltd. Used by permission. All rights reserved.

Page 41, From Frank Borman, *Life,* January 17, 1969. Copyright: Life Magazine, © 1972 Time Inc.

Page 42, From "A Reflection" by Archibald MacLeish. © 1968 by The New York Times Company. Reprinted by permission.

Pages 51, 84, 100, From *A Faith for This One World?* by Lesslie Newbigin. Copyright, 1961, by Lesslie Newbigin. Reprinted by permission of SCM Press Ltd.

Pages 90, 115, From Robert Raines, "The New-Time Religion," in the *Ladies' Home Journal,* December 1969. © 1969 Downe Publishing, Inc. Reprinted by permission of *Ladies' Home Journal.*

Page 93, From *While Gods Are Falling* by Earl Lovelace. Copyright, 1965, by Earl Lovelace. Reprinted by permission of Collins Publishers.

Page 94, From *Fetters of Injustice.* Quoted with permission from Archbishop Camara's address, "Development Projects and Concern for Structural Changes" to the Ecumenical Consultation on Development, Montreux, Switzerland, January 1970, printed in *Fetters of Injustice,* edited by Pamela H. Gruber (Geneva, WCC, 1970).

Pages 96, 101, 105, From Barbara Ward Jackson. Reprinted by permission of The World Publishing Company from *World Development:* Challenge to the Churches, edited by Denys Dunne. Copyright © 1969 by the Joint Committee on Society, Development and Peace.

Page 96, From "Warlords" by Gloria Maxson. Copyright 1972 Christian Century Foundation. Reprinted by permission from the February 16, 1972 issue of *The Christian Century.*

Pages 106-108, From *Partnership or Privilege?* Reprinted with permission of Sodepax from *Partnership or Privilege?* a Sodepax Report, Geneva, August 1970.

contents

preface

This book is addressed to every person who is searching for meaning in a time like this.

Many of the questions raised may appear at first to be the specialized concern of church bureaucrats and mission boards. But in fact these are basic issues facing the ordinary human being who is searching for a meaningful life in this complex global age.

This book arose out of an urgent need to know afresh the meaning of Christian mission in our time.

We are pressed in new ways with the question: "Why mission today?" This question comes out of at least four circumstances: (1) the perplexity of the ordinary individual about how to live as a human being in this strange new world age; (2) the uncertainty among Christians about Christian world mission; (3) the secular world's criticisms of historic missions; and (4) attacks on Western mission programs by people in the Third World, both Christians and others.

In the light of new things happening, it is urgent for churches to look again at the way each church, in its own situation and as part of the church universal, is participating in God's mission to the world.

Much of the content of this book has its source in a world mission consultation called in June 1971 by the Presbyterian Church in Canada, and a report I wrote of it, *For Such a Time as This*. The objective of that consultation was "to define the world mission task today in terms that are (1) authentic to the gospel, (2) real to the contemporary world, (3) firmly set in the realities of the world-wide church, and (4) meaningful for the involvement of the local congregation and its members."

The recurring and determining theme throughout the consultation was the question of how we understand salvation in the context of the contemporary world, and what our role is in relation to it. This led deeply into biblical study.

Throughout this book I have made extensive use of quotations from recent addresses and documents with the specific intent of introducing the reader to the creative discussions going on around the world.

I am also indebted to many other sources, not all specifically acknowledged, which have provided guides and encouragement.

I am well aware that this book is hardly more than an introduction to the study of profound questions facing mankind in our day. But I hope it may provide a small contribution to that world study and that it will be a useful introduction to this discussion for many who would not hear it otherwise.

I would express my gratitude to Miss Dawn Ross, editorial assistant and typist, through whose skill and dedication the writing of this book was completed and its publication facilitated.

E. H. Johnson
Toronto, Ontario
October, 1972

1

"now is the time"

"Shout for joy, you heavens, rejoice, O earth,
you mountains, break into songs of triumph,
for the Lord has comforted his people
and has had pity on his own in their distress."
—Isaiah 49:13, NEB

These triumphant words were God's response to his people at a time when they were complaining, "The Lord has forsaken me; my God has forgotten me."

In this moment of dark despair rang out the announcement of the Lord, "Now is the time: I will beckon to the nations and hoist a signal to the peoples."

"Things fall apart"

"Things fall apart," said W. B. Yeats.[1] We surely know what that means. During the past few decades our world has experienced the progressive and alarming breakdown of institutions and structures of society. Established ideas, traditional structures, and rules for living are all being questioned, and many have been discarded. Disorder and violence seem to reign. "Anarchy is loosed upon the world."

In the midst of collapse and confusion, of violence and counter-violence, of failure and frustration, people are fearful, perplexed, despairing. Some give up and drop out. Others carry on, hopeless of finding any real meaning. But some discern through the darkness the brilliant beams of the light of a new day.

Through the various revolutions of our time, the Holy Spirit is liberating men and women to enter into a life more fully human. All across the world, expressions are multiplying of new release of the human spirit. The anarchy and turmoil which appear to some as the death agonies of our world may indeed be the birthpangs of a new age.

This book declares that even in these times it is possible to be fully human and to live with hope. It declares the belief that God provides a way which gives joyful significance both to the life of the individual human person and to the history of mankind as a whole.

The God who is creator and Lord of all has sent Jesus Christ that men should not perish but have life, and has called the community of his people to be the special instrument of his triumphant, life-giving mission.

Over against the despairing cry, "Who will show us any good?" this book proclaims *it is a good time to be alive*. God is at work in human history, making all things new. Salvation is at hand. In the midst of perplexing and threatening events the clarion call is "Hoist a signal to the nations."

One great ground of hope

In 1942, when World War II was threatening to smash the "one world" just beginning to emerge, William Temple, in his enthronement sermon as Archbishop of Canterbury, spoke a discerning word: "As though in preparation for such a time as this, God has been building up a Christian fellowship which now extends into almost every nation, and binds citizens of them all together in true unity and mutual love. . . . Here is one great ground of hope for the coming days." [2]

In that critical moment for world development, Archbishop Temple discerned the world-wide Christian community as an instrument prepared for precisely "such a time." And he was able to declare in faith, "Here is one great ground of hope."

In the thirty years since that bold announcement, the world-wide Christian fellowship has made vast strides toward becoming an articulate, unified entity. Newly established churches have become rooted in newly formed nations and newly aware cultures. They have discovered their selfhood, broken ties of dependence on mother churches and established bonds of brotherhood and mutual service with the rest of the Christian community. They have explored ways of witness and discipleship related to their own cultures, and ways of service sensitive to their own needs. Within regional structures like the East Asia Christian Conference and the All Africa Conference of Churches they have discovered support, stimulation and insight into regional problems. The World Council of Churches itself has become a vital community through which the churches fulfill together their common calling.

If in 1942 Archbishop Temple could see the significance of the world-wide Christian fellowship, how much more can we today see it as "one great ground of hope," an instrument prepared by God "for such a time as this."

A world in transition

What are some of the characteristics of this time?

1. This is *a time of the actual emergence of a single world civilization.* It may well be the greatest single transi-

tion point in human history. Peoples of the world who lived for untold generations in what Lesslie Newbigin has called "the pools of non-historical existence and the rivulets of tribal history" are being drawn into the single current of world history. At this moment without precedent, every part of the world is being drawn irresistibly into a single "global village."

Within this one united world, our pasts and traditions are plural, but our future can only be singular. This one world civilization has been made possible and is the inevitable end result of Western science and technology.

The death agonies of our world may indeed be the birthpangs of a new age.

The way in which that driving Western technology has reached even to the most remote places was made vivid for me in a recent return visit to a tribal area in the hills of eastern India. The road, now paved, was paralleled by a power line bringing electricity from a distant dam, with smaller wires coming across the hills with the first telephone connection. A Burma Shell gasoline station stood at the crossroads, and Coca-Cola signs by the bus stop. These symbols of powerful coming events stood in sharp contrast to the ways of life of the tribal people. At night they still brought their cattle indoors with the family, and in the daytime still protected themselves with bows and arrows.

While for the West the whole world became familiar during the years of its world domination, for other peoples the fact and the reality of a single world civilization has become known only recently, if at all.

It is only since the late forties that most of the nations long held in colonial status and other forms of Western domination have gained political independence. But it is only within the early seventies that many peoples have been able to take effective part in world conversation. In 1971 and 1972 four of the world's great peoples—totaling almost half of the world's population—have come into more powerful participation in the world community.

The single most significant event was the entrance of the People's Republic of China into the United Nations in the autumn of 1971. This ended the impossible situation in which a nation containing a fifth of the world's people had no effective representation in what purported to be a world body. This event opens the possibility that some of the wisdom about development demonstrated in the restructuring of Chinese society may be shared with other areas, both "developed" and "developing," which are looking for ways of achieving a more equitable social and economic order.

In 1971 the explosive development of Japan as the world's third greatest trading nation led to major changes in trade agreements, with world-wide repercussions.

In early 1972 India was marked by a new mood of self-confidence. This sprang from solid agricultural and economic successes as well as new political stability. The catalyst which brought it to expression was victory in the "Fourteen Days War" with Pakistan, under the bold statesmanlike leadership of Indira Gandhi. Granted that the self-confidence was inflated by post-victory euphoria, and that vast economic and social problems still cry out for solution, India has experienced a confidence hardly known before, although it has enjoyed political independence for twenty-five years.

And in 1972 the new involvement of African peoples in world affairs was highlighted by the fact that the United

Nations Security Council met in Addis Ababa—the first time ever outside New York. In recent meetings, more than forty African nations acting together in the Organization of African Unity (OAU) have begun dealing with economic and other internal problems of Africa. In early 1972 it held the first All Africa Trade Fair, in Nairobi, and talked of forming an African economic community or trade bloc. The OAU also provides an articulate African voice in the international scene.

One may be sure that the voices of China and Japan and India and Africa will be raised with increasing force in the United Nations and other councils of the nations. The day of white domination has decisively ended, and the new day of a single world community is becoming a reality.

2. This is *a time of fear*. We fear for the survival of the human race. We are aware that continued abuse of our natural environment could have disastrous consequences for both nature and man. And we are also aware that the vast nuclear power built up to ensure our security might be accidentally triggered and launch a holocaust which could destroy the whole human race.

Yet it is also a time for hope. The same technology which threatens our destruction has the capability of solving many of our problems, *if* we can find the vision and the will to use it for conserving the environment and making peace.

3. This is *a time of glaring economic inequalities*. The gap between the rich and the poor nations is widening. These inequalities might continue without much difficulty in a world divided into isolated regions, but is intolerable in a unified world community. There is no way by which those who consider themselves the "plundered" can live content while those they see as the "pampered" enjoy a standard of life so much higher.

Yet it is a time for hope, for the affluent nations have a productive potential which, if equitably shared, could provide enough for all. While this is true, men of good will in the rich nations cannot accept the fact of undernourishment and poverty in the poor nations.

4. This is *a time of oppression.* There are still tens of millions who live as victims of or refugees from oppressive regimes. The rage of these people is growing and it will not be long before they will rise up in violent revolution, unless men of good will can in the meantime find ways of providing them full human rights.

Yet it is a time for hope, for men's consciences *are* being touched. The concern for a free life now protected for special races and groups, if extended to include the oppressed, could remove the tensions and allow men to join their strength in the common welfare and freedom of the whole.

5. This is *a time of religious pluralism,* in which many reborn religions are presenting competing claims. This has come about partly through the impact of Christianity, partly through the enlightenment of modern science and partly through the resurgence of national cultures. Those of other faiths are confident that their religious traditions provide the essential word for their own people. And many religions are making an increasingly explicit claim that they provide the answers for men everywhere. This kind of claim is being voiced now by Buddhism, Islam, Hinduism and also by many of the new faiths such as Baha'i, which claim to be more inclusive still. Many individuals, rejecting the older faiths, are trying to fill the vacuum by experiments in the occult and other novel religious practices which seem to offer understanding of the unknown.

Yet it is a time for hope. When men seek a single world faith, the light of the world cannot remain hidden. And human values embodied in the main religions and cultures of mankind can enrich the life of all.

6. This is *a time of lostness*. In this single world civilization we are all strangers, without compass or guidepost. Our previous life-styles, religious practices, political structures and basic assumptions are all inadequate. This is a problem no previous civilization has ever been called on to face.

It was once remarked by Hegel that in the Roman world, for the first time, the soul of man could be thoroughly lost. The tribal and community signposts which formerly gave men guidance were no longer adequate. How much greater that lostness is in our present situation.

While we have much of the technological equipment for journeying in this new land, we have lost our sense of direction. Everywhere man is casting about to find a way meaningful both for his inner life and for the world history which is the context of his life.

Yet, this very sense of lostness which marks our time is one of the most hopeful aspects of this moment, because it leaves men open for a word from the Lord to replace smaller voices no longer adequate.

Is the church really a "ground of hope"?

If these are some of the marks of our time, can it be said with any credibility that the world-wide Christian church has been prepared "for a time like this"? Can it be said that this fellowship is "the great new fact of our time," a "great ground of hope for the coming day"?

Many say no

Many outside the church answer with a resounding no. They do not take seriously the church's involvement in public affairs. Rather they see its concerns as spiritual and sentimental, neither concrete nor realistic. Others object to any claim of uniqueness as an expression of religious arrogance.

These outsiders are joined by many intelligent and educated people brought up within the Christian community who have now left it. Some have just drifted away, but others have impatiently rejected it.

This is a time of lostness. In this single world civilization we are all strangers.

These people have not found within the Christian community the vigor, excitement and power of the life-giving Christ about whom the community speaks. Nor have they met the rigorous demand of discipleship of the one who said, "Anyone who wishes to be a follower of mine must leave self behind."

Instead they have found the impoverished image of a Christ who has been tailored to the limitations of our Western culture. The magnificent vision of the Christ through whom God reconciles the whole universe to himself has been reduced to a narrow religiosity which does not meet the deep inner hunger of the individual nor his need for historical meaning in a world context.

Often the church has seemed more concerned with ecclesiastical privileges than with the welfare of mankind. It has seemed more concerned with religious activities than with human service.

Whenever in history the church moved away from God and substituted its own activities for a dynamic contemporary obedience, the judgment of God came upon it. It was carried into exile in Babylon, or taken to pieces, stone by stone, as was the temple in the early years of the Christian era. God has broken the man-made forms which have held the church captive, and has set it free to be the church, servant of his reconciling and saving mission to all the earth.

Others seek elsewhere

Those outside and those who have left the church because they feel it has no answer to the great questions of these times are searching elsewhere.

In many parts of the world that search has led them to communism and other political ideologies. In restructuring their societies, they have concentrated on technical and economic development, and have found personal meaning in total commitment to these objectives.

In our North American cities—particularly in the universities—people look for salvation in Hindu yoga, Zen Buddhism or other faiths. On Yonge Street in Toronto, Fifth Avenue in New York, Telegraph Street in Berkeley, young North Americans with saffron robes and shaven heads witness to their faith in Krishna. Some individuals experiment in witchcraft or in Satan worship, and in some of the lesser known Asian and Mediterranean practices. A scientist at the Massachusetts Institute of Technology—one of the world's great centers of scientific research—told me recently that one of the largest and most popular sections of the university bookstore was that on "the occult". And it is reported that in a major bookstore on New York's Fifth Avenue, books on the occult have crowded out from main counters traditional religious books, and these are now to be found in side spaces.

On a larger scale, the quest for identity has led to heightened expressions of nationalism or racism. The new nations of the world are jealous of their new national sovereignty. In the Caribbean they assert the rights of the "new Caribbean man". In Africa it is the "African fact". Among the black peoples in many parts of the world there is a vigorous announcement of "black theology," and of "black is beautiful". The people of China give single-minded attention to the teachings of Mao Tse-tung, and almost totally disregard other cultures and teachings. Surely we must accept this as the inevitable first reaction of peoples who have discovered their selfhood after generations when their culture was overwhelmed by the vigorous culture of the West.

Deep uncertainty even within the church

Many within the church find their answers in the Christian faith. But others have a very loose attachment to the church. Their faith often amounts to little more than a vague belief in some kind of God, with very little relation either to Jesus or to historic Christianity. And often what they believe is in strong contrast to the teachings of the church.

Church membership is often a casual and lightly held tie. Participation in worship is occasional, and the church is "used" mainly for baptism, marriage and burial services. Church membership is in many cases just a part of social respectability.

Christian identity is identification with the crucified one.

Even among faithful church members there is a deep uncertainty as to whether the church is "one great ground of hope for the coming day." They wonder if it really has a mission to this new world, or if it has the right to declare a faith to people of other cultures and other faiths. This all springs from a question about whether the Christian faith is so absolutely and finally true that we have a compelling obligation to share it with men and women of other faiths. In other words, many Christians are deeply uncertain about Jesus Christ and the dimensions of his authority.

Rediscovering our Christian identity

This widespread uncertainty, even within the church, concerning the Lordship of Christ and the relevance of the church drives us back to the biblical sources of our faith to examine afresh the meaning of God's salvation and the task of the church today.

The Christian community faces a crisis of its own Christian identity. We face the problem that while we proclaim Christ as Lord and Savior of all, we seem to stand on the fringe of rapidly changing events, an almost unheard voice.

At such a time, some try to establish contact with the times by attempting to make Christianity more relevant, by adjusting it to contemporary trends. Others go back to the forms of Christian expression prevalent when Christianity *was* effective in influencing society. But both of these are self-defeating, for both seek to adjust the living Christ to the ways of men, past or present.

God has called us as his people to be people of our age; and as people of our age to be fully his people. The question is not how to be modern or interesting, or how to recover old traditions, but only how to witness in a living way to our crucified and risen Lord. Christian identity is identification with the crucified one, and this involves us with all the peoples of the world.

Our need today is not to make faith relevant to the world, but rather to make the life and action of the church relevant to faith. It is not to attempt to substitute the action of man for the salvation of God, but rather to understand the salvation of God in all its fullness and to comprehend the proper role of the church in relation to his salvation.

2

salvation: where the action is

"What must I do to be saved?" is the urgent contemporary question, both of individuals and of all mankind. God's salvation, in all its multiple forms, is at hand.

Is there nothing to be done?

In Samuel Beckett's penetrating tragicomedy *Waiting for Godot,* the doubts and questions, the restless hopes and sense of futility of our day are voiced by the two main characters in various snatches of their conversation.

ESTRAGON: Nothing to be done.

VLADIMIR: I'm beginning to come round to that opinion. All my life I've tried to put it from me, saying, Vladimir, be reasonable, you haven't yet tried everything. And I resumed the struggle.

. . .

VLADIMIR: We've nothing more to do here.

ESTRAGON: Nor anywhere else.

VLADIMIR: Ah, Gogo, don't go on like that. Tomorrow everything will be better.

ESTRAGON: How do you make that out?

VLADIMIR: Did you not hear what the child said?

ESTRAGON: No.

VLADIMIR: He said that Godot was sure to come tomorrow. What do you say to that?

ESTRAGON: Then all we have to do is to wait on here.

. . .

ESTRAGON: I can't go on like this.

VLADIMIR: That's what you think. . . .
We'll hang ourselves tomorrow. Unless Godot comes.

ESTRAGON: And if he comes?

VLADIMIR: We'll be saved.[1]

. . .

Is nothing happening? Has no one come? Is there nothing to do?

More recently the contemporary mood may have been indicated by the great success in London and New York of the musical *Stop the World—I Want to Get Off*. People want to cop out from the fast pace of a world going nowhere. Better to disengage, live at your own speed, do your own thing. Better to escape from established institutions and traditional life-styles which prevent life from being fully human.

Without doubt the tremendous response to the Beatles lay partly in the fact that they voiced the deep cry of a lost generation.

Help! I need somebody.
Help! Not just anybody.
Help! You know I need someone.
HELP! [2]

Wanted: a living faith for a single world

The world at large is profoundly disillusioned with the powers in which it has trusted. Science, technology and managerial skill have performed miracles in solving particular problems, but have not been able to provide answers to the fundamental questions of quality and order in human life. They have often become tools which dehumanize life. And by making older faiths untenable they have left men with a spiritual vacuum.

Discerning thinkers now point out that the humanization of technology must come from the mystics, for the scientists and mechanists are too exclusively involved in their own processes. We need prophets and yogis and gurus. Increasingly, thinkers are recognizing that every great civilization has been built on a faith. The new world civilization is awaiting its faith and a community which expresses that faith and brings it to life.

Fresh winds are blowing

At this moment when in the world there is an urgent search for help coupled with a new openness, the church is coming up with exciting developments of insight and expression. Fresh winds of the Spirit are blowing. New things are happening, and there is a mood of expectation. Christians across the world are engaged in a deep-level search for fresh understanding of the Savior and his work in our contemporary world.

In the past, this sort of study has focused mostly on problems of church programing and structures. But now it has turned to basic questions concerning the faith and styles of life by which it can be expressed.

Much of today's study focuses on a word unpopular within

the church, the word salvation. Often it has been misused and distorted by groups claiming it for narrow sectarian purposes. To the layman it seems to suggest small and inverted religiosity with little relation to good news and abundant life.

Today the word is rediscovered and reexamined in all its biblical richness, and begins to reveal light as large as life and all the created universe. Here is the clue to what is going on in the world. Here is where the real action is.

Too long we have thought of salvation as being concerned mainly with the satisfaction of the individual soul within the limited realm of personal relationships. But in the Bible, salvation is concerned with "being right with God" in far wider terms. The God of salvation is also the God who intervenes in history in favor of his people. Salvation has political and physical as well as spiritual dimensions, and concerns every need of men and nations.

Salvation for all men now

It is indicative of the significant thought movements of our day that "Salvation Today" was the theme of the January 1973 conference in Bangkok, called by the Commission on World Mission and Evangelism of the World Council of Churches.

The preparatory statement for this conference reveals a fresh understanding of salvation which has emerged from years of study by groups in every part of the world. In the following passages taken from it, salvation is seen in its relation to the multiple needs of men everywhere.

Men struggle today for liberation from political, social and economic oppression. They seek release from suffering. They long to share in true human community, to discover some ultimate meaning transcending the alienation of human life. They look for peace, justice, freedom, wholeness, maturity, fulfillment and joy. All these traditional and contemporary terms are for Christians united in the word salvation, and through that word are related to the Saviour who is Jesus Christ.

This statement affirms that God's salvation is for all men. Christians have no monopoly on it.

For Christians, salvation is in Jesus Christ. There is no salvation apart from him; yet his salvation is for all men. Neither the word nor the hope of salvation belong to Christians alone. Indeed it is the theme of the scriptures of other faiths. It is also the theme of contemporary songs and plays. . . . Men and women of all kinds, in every land, use the word salvation and hope for it.

It is not an abstract concept, or religious activity, but is worked out in human life.

God's salvation is worked out in history. That is why Jesus came. The event of his life, death and resurrection was not only of local but of cosmic significance. Nor is it only a past event. It is what God is doing *today*.

Salvation belongs not to the past alone but is a continuing present activity of God.

We believe that God has acted and still acts. Jesus the Saviour is the focus of God's saving acts, who brought the world salvation by his incarnation, life, death and resurrection.

Through the Holy Spirit he is at work today, accomplishing God's purpose of salvation.

Salvation is a task in which God invites his people to participate, that men everywhere may enter into God's future fulfillment which already governs the present.

God's act today also demands a response. It becomes a contemporary experience continually renewed in faith. It gives hope and promise for the future. It sets men free today to fight against everything which frustrates the purpose of God. . . . Our task as Christians is to witness, through word and deed, to this work of Christ and his Spirit among us in today's world. This is the aim, . . . "to further the proclamation to the whole world of the Gospel of Jesus Christ, to the end that all may believe in Him and be saved." [3]

While these statements would appear to be an adequate declaration of a faith for living, it is important that they be tested against the actual hopes and fears today of men and women from all the world, and to explore whether these beliefs can in fact lead to new life-styles and decisive Christian action.

Finally, of course, our confidence is not in the correctness of our statements, or the force and skill of our action, but in the living Christ to whom we bear witness. We proclaim the one who said, "I shall draw all men to myself, when I am lifted up from the earth" (John 12:32). And after he had been crucified and had risen from the tomb, he declared, "Full authority in heaven and on earth has been committed to me" (Matthew 28:18b).

Biblical salvation is rich and wide

The word "salvation" appears in many contexts in both the Old and New Testaments. It has been seen differently in different periods by the people of Israel and the early Christian community. It relates to a wide variety of people and events. It is nowhere set forth in measured theological propositions, but appears rather within a record of the mighty acts of God.

Perhaps there is no word which expresses more fully the comprehensive richness of God's salvation than the Hebrew word *shalom.* This word includes righteousness, peace, community, integrity—all the gifts of the Messianic age and all aspects of human life in its full and God-given maturity. The Messiah is the prince of *shalom;* he shall be the *shalom;* the gospel is a gospel of *shalom;* the preaching of the apostles is summarized as preaching *shalom* through Jesus Christ. We are ambassadors to proclaim "now is the day of *shalom.*"

Deliverance is near to those who worship him.

—Psalm 85:9

Salvation, God's mission, the mission to which he calls every human being, is to cooperate with God in establishing the *shalom,* in which all creation shall realize its full potential through reconciliation and unity in Christ.

Eight affirmations about salvation

1. *God's salvation is for the whole of creation.* Biblical faith has an incredible vision of the Lordship of Christ. "In him everything in heaven and on earth was created, not

only things visible but also the invisible orders of thrones, sovereignties, authorities, and powers; the whole universe has been created through him and for him. And he exists before everything, and all things are held together in him" (Colossians 1:16–17).

God's salvation, then, is no less than the salvation and fulfillment of the whole universe and all its powers. And this is accomplished through the death and resurrection of Christ, "the first to return from the dead, to be in all things alone supreme. . . . Through him God chose to reconcile the whole universe to himself, making peace through the shedding of his blood upon the cross" (Colossians 1:18a, 20a).

The inclusion of the natural world within God's saving activity is declared in Romans, where the salvation of men and the fulfillment of the whole creation are joined as inseparable parts of one whole. "The universe itself is to be freed from the shackles of mortality and enter upon the liberty and splendor of the children of God. Up to the present, we know, the whole created universe groans in all its parts as if in the pangs of childbirth" (Romans 8:21–22). Man's failure to be a servant of God, working with him in his salvation, is expressed partly in his failure to be a good steward of God's earth.

2. *Salvation concerns the fact of individual suffering and sin.* Everyone needs a Savior. "All have sinned and come short of the glory of God." Biblical faith is thoroughly realistic about the pride and pretense, the guilt and insecurity, the torments of doubt and meaninglessness, and the enslaving anger and evil habits which lay their bondage on men.

Because Christ is Lord and Savior of all creation, his salvation is sufficient for all people no matter what the depth of their sin or the nature of their need. There is no hiding place beyond his judgment, no depth of lostness beyond his love and forgiveness.

Salvation brings to the individual a word of personal reconciliation with God and the hope of liberation from all the enslavements of human life. As the cross of Christ brings us starkly face to face with the reality and power of evil, so the resurrection reveals the victory and power of God. The cross and resurrection pronounce judgment on every source of despair and provide power for new life. And in this power the individual has hope of life becoming both what man longs for and what God intended.

3. *Salvation is victory over death.* Death has always been the one certainty we have about life. It is the common fact that ties together all members of the human race. At the moment of birth we begin the journey toward death. Whoever we are—young or old, man or woman, white or black—we are on that same journey. And when we reach the end, what lies beyond? Bliss, or torment, or nothingness? No matter how we try to mask death, or refuse to face it, it is the inexorable fact. It fills our hearts with uncertainties and fears and deep frustrations.

Salvation is God's action toward the whole creation realizing its full potential.

But at this particular moment in history, we have to contend not only with the reality of individual deaths—

which have always been with us—but also with the threat that the whole earth could be reduced to a heap of cold ashes. We need faith to carry us forward even in the face of that kind of annihilation.

The salvation of Christ declared the victory of life over death. In his resurrection death has been vanquished and life has conquered. He can declare, "I am the resurrection and I am life. If a man has faith in me, even though he die, he shall come to life; and no one who is alive and has faith shall ever die" (John 11:25–26).

In Christ we can go forward into all the risks of this new and perilous world. Even if all the earth should become a heap of cold ashes—what of that? God is not defeated. Death is beaten. There is a resurrection. This is the liberation, this is the salvation Christ brings to the world today.

4. *Salvation brings men into true community.* While salvation is personal it is never simply individual. It rescues the individual from alienation from himself, from God, and from his neighbor, and brings him into right relationships.

To accept Christ as Savior is to accept him also as Lord. To accept his sovereignty is to become part of the body of Christ, to be brought into unity with his people and with all mankind. It is to take part in his saving action for all men. The saved person will serve his Lord in working to overthrow the forces of evil within and around men that separate them from their creator and from each other, that human life may discover its nature in communion with God.

5. *Salvation concerns liberation for all people from every oppression.* How often throughout the Bible is God's salvation described in terms of liberation from captivity, and his people exhorted to release the oppressed.

In both the Old and New Testaments, justice and liberation of the oppressed are an ever present theme. In biblical faith one cannot separate between spiritual liberation and social justice, for both are part of God's salvation.

In Exodus and Deuteronomy, Israel is instructed to keep the commandments, remembering it was God's "strong hand and outstretched arm" that had brought them out of slavery in Egypt. "It was because the Lord loved you and stood by his oath to your forefathers, that he brought you out with his strong hand and redeemed you from the land of slavery. . . . Know then that the Lord your God is God, the faithful God" (Deuteronomy 7:8–9a).

This event of liberation from enslavement became for Israel the single most decisive and oft-recalled sign of God's loving grace and mighty power. To this day when the Jewish people gather for Passover, they recall that moment of liberation.

In the fifth chapter of Amos, the prophet voices God's disgust at those who "turn justice upside down and bring righteousness to the ground," and his disdain for their worship. "I hate, I spurn your pilgrim-feasts; I will not delight in your sacred ceremonies. . . . Spare me the sound of your songs." And in those great words which have echoed across the centuries he exhorts his people: "Let justice roll on like a river and righteousness like an ever-flowing stream."

God still calls his people to free the oppressed, whether they be oppressed by racism or capitalism or communism or any other form of tyranny. God still scorns the complacent worship of his people when they do nothing about the injustice and oppression inflicted on their fellow men, for liberation is a primary element of the salvation worship celebrates.

6. *God has called out a people as an instrument of his salvation.* In the Old Testament, Israel was a people called out, through whom all the nations of mankind might be blessed. Peter speaks of the New Testament church as "a chosen race, a royal priesthood, a dedicated nation, and a people claimed by God for his own, to proclaim the triumphs of [the Christ]" (1 Peter 2:9).

The first public act of Jesus noted in the Gospel of Mark is the establishment of a community of disciples who remained with Jesus throughout his ministry. Their encounter in Galilee with the risen Lord may be interpreted as a sign of their importance in the total saving work of Jesus. His post-resurrection words as recorded in the Gospels ("Go forth therefore and make all nations my disciple"), and in the book of Acts ("You will bear witness for me in Jerusalem, and all over Judaea and Samaria, and away to the ends of the earth") testify to the particular role the community of the people of Jesus Christ has to play.

The church is a fellowship called out, but it is not a fellowship which isolates us from the rest of mankind or from the life of the world. Rather we are called out of the isolation of one family and one nation and one race, to be fully a part of all humanity and all creation. We are called to be the servant of God's saving purposes for all things.

7. *God works out his salvation not only through the church but also outside and beyond the church.* The Bible is full of instances of God's saving power reaching outside the circle of his chosen people. Jesus incurred the wrath of his kinsmen in Nazareth when he emphasized that God's grace had come to a widow of Sarepta (in Sidon), rather than to a widow of Israel, and that his healing power had come to Naaman the Syrian general rather than to a leper in Israel.

The Bible also records many events in which God acted through individuals and peoples who did not know him. For example, Cyrus, the Persian ruler, is nevertheless spoken of as the Lord's "anointed." To Cyrus, God said: "You shall be my shepherd to carry out all my purpose, so that Jerusalem may be rebuilt and the foundations of the temple may be laid" (Isaiah 44:28). It was Cyrus, conqueror of Babylon and many lesser nations, who permitted the Jews to return from captivity in Babylon to their own land, and to rebuild the temple there. To him the Lord said, "I have called you by name and given you your title, though you have not known me" (Isaiah 45:4).

Whoever wants to limit salvation to the activities of the organized church or to the "circle of the pious" is putting fetters on the Holy Spirit. The Spirit takes the liberty to include in his action both Christians and non-Christians, even when many of them do not know the name of Christ or even reject him.

This is a hard truth for the church to accept. We like to feel that we have the Christ in our hands, rather than accept the fact that we, along with all mankind, are in the hands of the Christ and can be rejected by him when we are disobedient or unfaithful.

An essential part of the Christian's task is to discern the saving activity of God in the world beyond the organized church, and to respond at the places where God is breaking through in human history.

8. *The power of salvation is always God's.* While the church is called for mission, the power is always of God and not of men. It is the Holy Spirit that saves, not our evangelistic programs. Mission is never the church's own, but always remains the mission of God. The church may be the instrument God uses to save men, but the power that

saves is not in the instrument: it is in the hand of the One who uses the instrument.

Respond at the places where God is breaking through in human history.

When we understand that salvation is God's activity, we recognize that it is not a static concept but a dynamic reality. We play our part in a process which is taking place now and which is yet to be completed, reaching beyond the boundaries of death.

Knowing that the mission is God's, we can go out into the world to play our part with joy and confidence. We will not, like Atlas, try to carry on our own shoulders the world and all its burdens. Rather we will celebrate and give thanks for a salvation which is not man's. It is God who planned it, it is God who empowers it and it is God who will fulfill it in his own good time.

The Lord is at hand

One cannot leave the theme of salvation without asking the question, when? When will the individual find release and fulfillment? When will the new society of justice and peace replace our present society, with all its wrongs and strife?

In biblical faith, *shalom* belongs to the Messianic era, when the Christ establishes his rule. That era has now come. The future belongs to Christ, and that future determines the present, even though the present still has its problems. The writer of Ephesians speaks of the vast resources of Christ's power now open to those who trust in God. "They are measured," he says, "by his strength and the might which he exerted in Christ when he raised him from the dead, when he enthroned him at his right hand in the heavenly realms, far above all government and authority, all power and dominion, and any title of sovereignty that can be named, not only in this age but in the age to come" (Ephesians 1:19–21).

The Christian does not live by faith in the utopian ideal that human woes and conflicts will all vanish. Such a faith is belied by the continuation of turmoil. Rather he lives in realistic confidence about the final outcome made known in the resurrection of the Christ. With confidence in Christ's vast power and final victory, the Christian has courage to play a resolute and constructive role in the midst of the shocks and failures and betrayals of the present. He can bring this hope of the future, already revealed, to bear on the burdens and anxieties of the present.

The Christian is one who lives for the future which in Christ has begun here and now. To men who are paralyzed from taking action by fear of the future, the Christian declares hope and triumph already manifest in Christ. As part of Christ's triumphal procession he lives as a member of the new humanity of the God who says, "Behold, I make all things new." In faith in the Christ and his salvation he goes out into the world in a mood of thankful wonder, joyous expectancy and buoyant confidence.

On the frontier we see our Savior is "beautiful"

To help us understand the affirmations in Ephesians and Colossians about the greatness of Christ's sovereignty and salvation, we should know that the man who wrote them lived on the frontier of the Christian community, and that he wrote them late in his life.

Paul was not a member of an established congregation within a Christian culture in which the churches are the accepted "religious" expression of the culture. Day after day he himself had to interpret the meaning of his gospel. He had no New Testament records to sustain him, but only word-of-mouth reports about Jesus, his own knowledge of and reflections on the Old Testament, his experience of Christ on the Damascus road and the witness of fellow believers.

He was exposed—completely exposed—to the thoughts, the faiths, the ideologies, the economic pressures, the criticisms, the abuse of those around him. He was constantly forced back on the question: What is this gospel? Who is this Christ who is leading me? And out of that experience of loneliness and constant attack, Paul discovered the unsearchable riches of Christ.

In recent years, we Christians in the West have lived in a protected world, where there has been almost no pressure of other faiths, and where our civilization has for the most part totally accepted our role and function as the church. We have been deprived of the sort of living confrontation Paul had.

But in more recent years as the Christian faith has been planted in the Third World, the forms and traditions of Western Christianity have often been exposed as quite inadequate. In this one world civilization we are all once more on the frontier.

As we stand once again in an exposed position we may have to face again, day after day, the same sort of challenge Paul did. But, unlike Paul, we face it now as part of a great company of Christians from many lands and cultures.

If we have the honesty and courage to expose ourselves to the challenge, we may be driven back from the Christs we have designed in our own image and clothed in our own cultural garb, to the remarkable figure of Christ the Lord, in all of his world-encompassing love and power and glory. In him we will discover everything we need "for a time like this."

3

no longer strangers but fellow citizens

Called from every race and nation,
we live now in the ecumenical era,
no longer strangers
but fellow citizens with the saints.

Our global home—moon's eye view

The fact that our world is one was made real to us in an unforgettable experience at Christmastime 1968, when we shared with the Apollo 8 astronauts a spectacular view of our global home as a whole. The tragic realities of that one world were deeply etched on our minds by the words of Frank Borman describing what was so obvious from the moon.

It was hard to think that that little thing held so many problems, so many frustrations. Raging nationalistic interests, famines, wars, pestilence don't show from that distance. I'm convinced that some wayward stranger in a spacecraft, coming from some other part of the heavens, could look at earth and never know that it was inhabited at all. But the same wayward stranger would certainly know instinctively that if the earth *were* inhabited, then the destinies of all who lived on it must inevitably be interwoven and joined.[1]

Archibald MacLeish captures the impact for mankind of this event in the few lines:

> To see the earth as it is, small and blue and beautiful in that eternal silence where it floats, is to see ourselves as riders on the earth together, brothers in that bright loveliness in the eternal cold—brothers who know now that they are truly brothers.[2]

Most of us are still hardly aware that we are now in a new ball game in which the rules and practices of the old game are no longer adequate. Modern technology has tied us together in ways from which we can never be quite separated.

In 1965 Arnold Toynbee pointed out that "Until now, nearly all human beings have divided their fellows into two groups: a minority group which is our kith and kin, and a majority group which is outsiders, aliens and potential enemies." But now that modern technology has annihilated distance, "we have to take the whole human race into the fold of our kith and kin, behaving to all men as we have behaved in the past only to members of our own minority group: our family, our nation, our church." [3]

The question of life today is basically the question of what it means to be human beings in this age when the life and problems of people in one area are so drastically affected by, and in turn affect, the life and problems of people in every other area.

A world-wide fellowship prepared for such a moment

It is fortunate that at this moment when we enter global community there exists a world-wide community which already has experienced fellowship and common work across almost every boundary of race and nation.

In his memorable enthronement sermon (quoted in Chapter I), the former Archbishop of Canterbury describes this fellowship as "the great new fact of our time" and "one great ground of hope for the coming days." But Archbishop Temple was realistic enough to know that this is a resource whose full potential will flow only when all the members of the fellowship become aware of it and make practical use of its myriad possibilities. "It is of urgent importance," he said, "that we become aware of [this world-wide fellowship], that we further it in every way open to us, and that through it we take our part in providing for the Spirit of God the agency by which he may transform the world." He saw the recognition and expression of unity in the church as serving the purpose of God for the unity of mankind.

In the New Testament the church itself is spoken of as a kind of preliminary model, on a small and imperfect scale, of what the final state of mankind is to be in God's design. It is treated as both the first fruits of God's work and the promise of the future.

Back in the second century an early church father spoke of Christians as the soul of the world, holding it together in unity. His words speak to us with amazing relevance today:

> What the soul is in the body Christians are in the world. The soul is spread through all the members of the body; so are Christians through all the cities of the world. . . . The soul is enclosed within the body, and itself holds the body together; so too Christians are held fast in the world as in a prison, and yet it is they who hold the world together.[4]

If that statement was true when the church was a tiny minority within the great Roman Empire, how much more is it true when the church embraces within its membership people of every nation and race, and stands alone as such a community.

A report from a World Council of Churches conference highlights the tremendous potential for world community in the existence of the world-wide Christian fellowship.

If men and women are to find the faith and courage to co-operate with God in the struggle for tomorrow's world, they need to see and feel what it is like to live in an international, multi-racial, trans-cultural community. It is the calling of the churches to make such a community experience a reality.[5]

In the summer of 1972 a news release from Peking illustrated vividly the new kind of possibilities latent in this world-wide fellowship. The headline ran, "AFRICANS CROWD PEKING CHURCHES" and the release went on to say:

Peking's two Christian churches—one Protestant and the other Roman Catholic—were crowded yesterday for the first time since the start of the cultural revolution in 1966. The congregations were comprised mainly young Africans from Tanzania and Zambia who arrived in China recently for a three-year course in railway engineering. China is helping to build a railway linking the two African countries. About forty students attended a Protestant service in an old Chinese-style hall and a Zambian student said a lesser number went to mass in the Catholic church. Religion has been discouraged in China since the Communists came to power in 1949 and the churches closed down altogether during the turbulent years of the cultural revolution.[6]

Christians around the world have wondered how fellowship with Christians in China might be reestablished. No one wanted to take initiatives which might offend the Chinese people and embarrass Chinese Christians. Who would have guessed that one of the first contacts in public worship would be Africans from a former colonial area, not clergy but laymen, brought to China by the Chinese themselves?

When God has prepared this new instrument for this global day, his people need the sensitivity, imagination and expectancy to respond to his initiative.

We live in the ecumenical era

The word "ecumenical" comes from the Greek *oikoumene,* which means "the whole inhabited earth." It has become known mostly through what has been called "the ecumenical movement," in which the churches have tried to find appropriate expression for the basic fact of their given oneness in Christ. This movement, which had its deep sources in the world missionary movement, has taken hold in the last fifty years. The World Council of Churches has drawn together more than 260 churches—Anglican, Protestant and Orthodox—into a fellowship to fulfill together their common calling. Conversations are in progress with the Roman Catholics, and World Council and Roman Catholic agencies with shared concerns undertake many joint projects.

We have to take the whole human race into the fold of our kith and kin.

—Arnold Toynbee

"Ecumenical" should never be confused with "interdenominational." The latter puts emphasis on the particular fellowships which men have constructed at particular times and places. The former emphasizes that the church which is God's creation is one, called by him and always dependent on him for power and fulfillment.

The word "ecumenical" has integrity only in terms of the whole Christian community. That which is ecumenical is strictly evangelical, for the oneness of the church flows from the unity of the gospel. And evangelical implies ecumenical, for trust in the one gospel can result only in one church. We all stand within the wholeness of that one humanity which God has created, and that one grace by which we are brought into his church.

The swift transition from the familiar, protected situation of Christendom into the new exposed context of the *oikoumene* is confusing and frustrating for many people. We no longer live within a nice, safe world of national sovereignties—a world within which biblical faith was always ill at ease—but in the context of the whole of God's creation and his purpose of love for the whole of mankind, a situation within which biblical faith is fully at home. Ecumenism really derives its meaning from the book of Genesis. There we learn that all men were created by one God, and that Abraham was called so that he and his people might be a blessing for all mankind.

In the New Testament era, the word "ecumenical" took on a new reality at Pentecost. The Holy Spirit came "like the rush of a mighty wind," and men began to speak in other tongues, each hearing the other in his own language. The Holy Spirit speaks in a language each man recognizes as his own.

Over the years I have been privileged to experience the universal at-home-ness of Jesus Christ in many languages and circumstances. In great cathedrals in many parts of the world I have joined in the prayer of our Lord, and it has seemed the authentic and original prayer in each. In humble peasant homes in the villages of India, among the mountain tribes of Taiwan and in floodlands of Guyana, with livestock and poultry sharing the dwellings, I have joined in the Lord's Prayer and it has seemed the authentic and original word for those places. In the power of the Spirit these people have heard the word of God as a word in their own language, and have discovered that the prayer of our Lord is in truth the prayer of the human family.

The Holy Spirit speaks in a language each man recognizes as his own.

The deep and authentic meaning of "ecumenical" lies in the basic unity of Christ's church as one household. We are not many; we are one. And this is not because of our unity movements but by God's creation. The movement toward expressing the given unity of the church is not primarily for ecclesiastical goals but for human goals. The study of church unity is being made not only in the context of divided denominations but in the wider context of the divisions of mankind. Is the world-wide Christian community not "a sign of the coming unity of mankind"?

Two cautions

The emergence of our global society and the great new fact of the world-wide Christian community are occasions for rejoicing. But even as we receive and celebrate them we should be aware of two historic facts.

1. *Our "one world" has only just emerged from an era in which the whole of mankind was subjugated by the "Christian" nations of the West.*

In his book *The World and the West,* Arnold Toynbee says that the West has been the arch-aggressor of modern times, that each non-Western people has its story to tell of Western aggression.[7]

In 1492 Christopher Columbus, on a voyage to find the direct route to India and the rich plunder of Asia, discovered the West Indies and the Americas. From that time, European nations took over the largely empty continents of North and South America, and the story was an ugly one. In North America, native peoples were ruthlessly hunted down, their lands appropriated and their way of life destroyed. In the Caribbean and Central and South America, brutal hardship, military excesses and Western diseases, for which the natives had no resistance, destroyed millions of the original populations. Occasional voices, usually those of churchmen like the Spanish monk Las Casas, were raised against the excesses, but the plunder went on.

When the new conquerors needed cheap labor to exploit their vast new territories, they began the slave trade to the Americas. Millions of people from the west coast of Africa were carried across the Atlantic in slave ships in indescribable misery and sold like animals to work the plantations of white European owners. This terrible blot on history of man's inhumanity to man was part of the rule of the New World by the "Christian" nations of western Europe.

In 1498 Vasco da Gama achieved his historic voyage around the southern tip of Africa to India. Thus began the series of ruthless attacks which gradually subjugated the whole of eastern Asia. All of India, Ceylon, Indonesia, Southeast Asia and finally the vast nations of China and Japan were brought under the political, economic or military control of the nations of the West and were often treated as pawns to be traded about in the power struggles of Europe. Their riches laid the foundations of the vast affluence of the West, while the East continued in poverty.

The story, though marked occasionally by some great and generous figures and by some acts and policies showing real concern for human welfare, was for the most part characterized by greed and brutality. The Eastern nations, many of whose civilizations were far ahead of Europe at that time, were profoundly hurt. One cannot overestimate the humiliation suffered by the peoples of India and China through this dominion by people regarded as barbarians.

Late in the nineteenth century Europe established an almost total domination over the continent of Africa, and again the story is one of brutality and ruthless unconcern for the welfare and feelings of the subjugated peoples.

We should not forget that the world has come into the ecumenical era not by the gentle growth and establishment of relationships across the various barriers of race and civilization, but by years of violence in which the white world set out to dominate all the world, and did in effect establish a world community of sorts, but under Western rule.

Only within the last twenty-five years, more than three-quarters of mankind has moved from political domination to political freedom: India and Pakistan in 1947, Indonesia in 1948, the People's Republic of China in 1949. Most of the African countries achieved political independence only in the sixties and so are barely ten years old. We have already seen that it is only in the last two or three years that some of the world's major nations have attained self-confidence and entered fully into the world conversation. Our "one world" has only just been born. We may expect some growing pains.

2. *The world-wide Christian fellowship itself has become a reality only recently.*

If we are to respond rightly to the exciting new world mission possibilities opened up by the new fact of world-wide Christian fellowship, we need to be aware of what this fellowship is at this stage. Some limitations and problems are natural results of its very recent birth.

It was almost 250 years after Christopher Columbus and Vasco da Gama before Protestant missions began as a continuing movement. Before this there had been a number of individual and group efforts in mission outreach, but these were often isolated and short-lived.

Between 1792 and 1824 at least twelve Protestant missionary societies were founded in Great Britain and North America. Most of these were voluntary and independent, not an integral part of church structures. Church authorities regarded missions often with cool disinterest and sometimes with open hostility. But the Holy Spirit raised up within the church new instruments to fulfill the church's purpose: the proclamation of the gospel to the whole world. From these small beginnings developed the great foreign missionary movement and missionary vision articulated by the early watchword of the Student Volunteer Movement: "The evangelization of the world in this generation." And from this movement, the church was planted around the world.

It was not until 1910 that the world missionary gathering which developed into what later became called "the ecumenical movement," convened in Edinburgh. Out of this gathering grew the International Missionary Council, formed of Christian Councils of nations in many parts of the world. In 1948, largely out of this initiative, the World Council of Churches came into being. In 1961 the International Missionary Council was merged with the World Council of Churches, for it was recognized that the church and its mission cannot be separated. Within the World Council, the

Commission on World Mission and Evangelism has given particular attention to the issues of world mission.

Only very recently have our churches begun to break free from church structures of Christendom, largely inward-looking, to discover anew the essential missional nature of the church. Lesslie Newbigin in his *A Faith for This One World?* has explained the background of the largely non-missional self-understanding characterizing churches:

I do not think that we reflect sufficiently upon the fact that most of the fundamental forms of our churchmanship were laid down during a period in which Christianity was a contracting and not an expanding religion, the period in which, hemmed in by the power of Islam and isolated from the great non-Christian cultures of the East, Christendom almost lost the consciousness of the world which was still waiting to be evangelized. . . . Christendom had become a self-contained world; the sense that the Church is a body sent into all the world, a body on the move and existing for the sake of those beyond its own borders, no longer played an effective part in men's thinking.

This fact is reflected in the fundamental forms of our church life. The ministry is conceived almost exclusively in pastoral terms as the care of souls already Christian. The congregation is seen as a body existing for the edification and sanctification of its own members rather than for witness and service to the world outside. Our very systems of doctrine tend to be constructed *vis-à-vis* other Christian systems, rather than *vis-à-vis* the great non-Christian systems of thought. And the normal content of a course in Church history has far more of the mutual disputes of Christians than of the missionary advances of the Church and the encounter of the gospel with the non-Christian cultures which it has successively met.[8]

As we live in the global community, as part of the world-wide Christian fellowship, we need to remember that both are still being formed.

Finding new structures for the new era

Confronted by the reality of a single world community, we need rigorously to examine attitudes and structures of our world outreach in the past. This is a moment of unprecedented possibilities, but also of new difficulties and hazards. It demands of God's people everywhere the humility and flexibility to leave behind what is no longer meaningful, and the courage and imagination to devise new patterns and structures of obedience.

We now have the possibility of receiving valuable insights from Christians of other cultures. Bishop R. S. Bhandare, deputy moderator of the newly formed Church of North India, shared some of his thinking with a recent consultation on world mission:

> We have discovered the ecumenical nature of our mission. It is not an invention but only a discovery because it has always been there: "in Jerusalem, and all over Judaea and Samaria, and away to the ends of the earth." It is not a successive or geographical mission; it is a simultaneous mission. The mission in which Christians all over the world are called to participate is God's mission. It is not a mission of a particular denomination nor is it a mission of churches here or churches there. It is the mission of the people of God throughout the world.[9]

He and his fellow Christians in India have felt deeply that much of the orientation of the church there is foreign; its practices and structures were brought from the West and planted in India, rather than being allowed to grow as a natural product of India's soil. Thus they look more like colonies of the West than "colonies of heaven."

> The forms of worship we have, the architecture of our church structures, the seating arrangements in our worship

sanctuaries, the dress of our people, the ministers as they go into the pulpit with shoes and all, and the paid ministry are not indigenous, are not according to the religious traditions of our country. The structures of the church, such as sessions, presbyteries, synods, general assemblies, moderators, metropolitans and canons, are never found in the religious traditions of India.

While emphasizing the importance of the Indian church discovering its self-identity within India, he underlined certain essential features of ecumenical relationships.

The time has come for us to look at our resources together, as stewards of the body of Jesus Christ. Unless we receive we cannot give, and unless we give we cannot receive. And the giver is one who is the creator of the world. When we give, let there be humility and stewardship. When we receive, let there be humility and stewardship.

Ecumenical planning means coming together, looking at the needs of the world together, and projecting our plans and sharing our resources. It is high time for us to look at the structures through which we channel our resources for participation in God's mission. It should be the grass roots of a church here related to the grass roots of a church elsewhere.

The leaders of the Korean Christian Church in Japan, a small minority church, have expressed what the ecumenical fellowship means to them. They see it not as an organizational structure imposing uniform practices, but rather as a unity within which all the diverse cultures and tongues can have expression and enrich the whole. They have written:

The incarnation of the gospel which is the driving force within the message of Christ, leads both to the rooting of the church within its own culture and society, and at the same time its full involvement as a unit of the church universal. The unique cultural manifestations of the church play against the essential unity of the gospel message. Without this tension, the dynamics of the gospel are lost.[10]

In a unique way they have discerned the value of the interplay between the necessity that each church become flesh and blood in a particular culture and place, and the fact that each church is at the same time a part of the one holy catholic church in all the world. This interplay will contribute to the building up of "the unity inherent in our faith and our knowledge of the Son of God—to mature manhood measured by nothing less than the full stature of Christ" (Ephesians 4:13).

Now the church exists everywhere in the world, and many leaders in the non-Western churches, conscious of their own cultures and nationalisms, feel that the missionary task now belongs to them. This is a time when the priorities and emphases are shifting from the organized, outgoing mission to the "mission through being" of every Christian community.

Some Christian individuals in the Third World feel strongly the time has come to terminate the organized missionary program from the West. One of the most outspoken of these is John G. Gatu, secretary of the Presbyterian Church of East Africa. At the beginning of an address given in Milwaukee in 1971 he said:

> I am going to argue that the time has come for the withdrawal of foreign missionaries from many parts of the "Third World," that the churches of the "Third World" must be allowed to find their own identity and that the continuation of the present missionary movement is a hindrance to this selfhood of the church.[11]

Gatu feels that both money and missionaries are a potential danger to the African church at this time. He quotes a contemporary writer who has said, "Men and money sent with missionary motivation carry a foreign Christian image, a foreign pastoral approach and a foreign political image."

He realizes that the church in Africa can still use foreign money and foreign personnel, but he feels that the basic need is for *more* than men and money, that it is for self-reliance.

We cannot build the church in Africa on "alms given by overseas churches." . . . The need is commitment and a decision to go forward in faith, for Africa has money and personnel, and until we have produced the "two loaves and five fishes," our Lord continues to say, "Give them something to eat."

He suggests at least a temporary break in relationships:

The answer to our present problems can only be solved [*sic*] if all missionaries can be withdrawn in order to allow a period of not less than five years for each side to rethink and formulate what is going to be the future relationship.

In July 1972 at a Geneva conference on the Ecumenical Sharing of Personnel, Gatu's thoughts were formulated into an actual proposal for a five-year moratorium on all sending of personnel and funds by Western mission agencies. While this proposal has far from unanimous support by African, Asian and other churches, it will be given careful study as a possible route to a self-reliance in which the churches may find a fresh vitality and joy.

In recent years there have been rapid and substantial changes in the relationships between the missionary sending organizations and the churches with whom they work. The younger churches are assuming increasing responsibility for their work, and mission agencies are playing only an enabling role. Personnel are moving in many directions, and the possibilities of ecumenical sharing of personnel are being explored.

The question is, how can we use to full advantage for

each place the rich and varied gifts of people from every place? And more important, how can the church in each place, as a local unit of the church universal, be the missionary for that place?

Mission through being and mission through going

In biblical witness, mission appears in two forms. The first is through the life and witness of God's people. Israel in the Old Testament was to be a witness to the nations. By its very existence and life-style it was to reflect God's mercy and glory, and thus to illumine the Gentiles. This was *mission through being,* through living in the grace and peace and freedom and joy of the Lord.

The second is the *outgoing mission.* It had been present in the servant concept of Isaiah: "My servant, whom I uphold . . . will bring forth justice to the nations. . . . He will not fail or be discouraged till he has established justice in the nations" (Isaiah 42:1-4a). It was strengthened by the imperative of the New Testament, "Go forth therefore and make all nations my disciples" (Matthew 28:19a).

How can the church in each place, as a local unit of the church universal, be the missionary for that place?

During the past two hundred years the world missionary activity of the church has been marked by the predominance of the "outgoing mission," which planted the church around the world. But this outgoing mission, begun by men and women who felt personally called to carry the gospel to the ends of the earth by word and compassionate deed, led to the establishment of large and powerful organized missionary structures.

Those structures are now being radically altered in the new context of the world Christian community and the new emphasis on the mission through being of every church.

People's power under the Holy Spirit

As we go forward in mission in this day, decisions about mission should not be taken unilaterally but only *in conversation with the rest of the world.* We now have structures through which such multilateral conversations can be made, but are only now discovering ways to use them.

Whatever new missionary patterns are developed, they should be *appropriate to the new sociological realities* of the contemporary world, and should be more than simply a copy of old forms of missionary presence, simply moving in the reverse direction. Someone has suggested a guerrilla structure of missionary presence, where small temporarily constituted groups create a process that is not easily destroyed. For the real power for conversion of individuals and of structures is the people's power, under the Holy Spirit.

We have a firm biblical basis for people's mission in the quotation from the prophet Joel in Acts 2:17–18: "God says, 'This will happen in the last days: I will pour out upon everyone a portion of my spirit; and your sons and daughters shall prophesy; your young men shall see visions, and your old men shall dream dreams. Yes, I will endue even my slaves, both men and women, with a portion of my spirit, and they shall prophesy.' "

In times past we have counted on the establishment: theological professors, church officials, women leaders, ordained ministers and elders. Let us not forget that God used William Carey, a cobbler, to call the church to a world-embracing task and to give prophetic leadership in many aspects of that task.

At this time when much of the missionary and evangelistic work of the establishment produces few results, we should welcome the new insights and prophetic vision of the younger generation and of the old, of both men and women, of people in every level of life. We should look to these often neglected sources for new insights and prophetic vision.

In this era of the Spirit let us live with great expectancy knowing that everyone may receive a portion of God's Spirit. From the children, from the young people, from the old, from the humblest workers will come the prophecies and dreams and visions to lead us into the coming years.

4

dialogue: a way of witness

Dialogue with men of other faiths and ideologies is a journey of exploration in the belief that the Holy Spirit guides men into all truth.

The religious encounter is happening now

More than ten years ago, John A. Mackay, then chairman of the International Missionary Council, warned us: "Christianity, Christians, and the Christian Church are now headed for the greatest spiritual encounter with the non-Christian religions since the days of the Roman emperor, Constantine." [1]

That encounter has already begun, for through modern transportation methods and revolutionary events, people of every nation and race and religion have been distributed in every part of the world. No longer do we need to go abroad to encounter other faiths. In early autumn, when Hindus observe their most sacred day, *Diwali,* more than a thousand Hindus gathered to celebrate in one of the high schools of Toronto—and they represented only a small part of the fourteen thousand Hindus then living in that city. And all the other major world faiths have groups in Toronto.

Wherever we live today, we live in a place of religious pluralism, and we need to prepare ourselves to hear what other religions have to say.

Secular education has already begun to take account of the spread of other religions and the importance of understanding them. Ontario's Department of Education in 1971 launched an experiment in studies in world religions for senior high-school students. It provides guides for studies of Hinduism, Buddhism, Judaism, Christianity and Islam.

The stated aim of the course is "the development of a sympathetic understanding of the meaning of different religions and their effect on the life and thought of their adherents." And at another level the study aims "to help the student to clarify his thinking on some of the fundamental questions about himself, and his relationship to his fellow man, to the universe and to the concept of a transcendent order." [2]

When the world was dominated by the West, it was assumed that Christianity would eventually prevail everywhere. Other religions were attacked as evil, or ignored as unimportant, or highly praised as superior and lightly quoted by intellectuals. The Christian church has been slow to decide what position to take in regard to other faiths.

What can we learn from other faiths?

Across the world, one finds a wide variety of ways in which men seek to share in truly human community and discover ultimate meaning for their lives. Some peoples follow highly sophisticated religions; others reject religion and establish instead a purely secular, humanistic society. But all are seeking the same end, a "salvation" which will give them peace, joy, justice and fulfillment.

Many years ago, as a young missionary in a somewhat isolated situation in central Manchuria, I had the opportunity to study Chinese religions as part of my introduction to Chinese language and culture. During that period of loneliness and difficult adjustment to a totally alien culture, I found great personal help in the *Book of Mencius* (one of the *Four Books* of the Confucian classics), in teachings of Taoism in the *Tao Te Ching* and of Buddhism in the *Lotus* and *Diamond* classics.

In the actual practices of the local Buddhist and Taoist temples and in some of the Confucian ceremonial practices, there was much that repelled rather than helped. But in the teachings of these faiths, and in the devotion and intensive search of some of their teachers and priests, I received an inspiration and personal encouragement badly needed at that time. I learned too that part of my task as a missionary of Christ was to be open to the word of truth which might come through another faith, but which had its origin in the One who is the source of all truth.

In more recent years in visits to Japan I have been deeply impressed by the calmness and serenity of some of its Buddhist temples and Shinto shrines. My first visit to the Ryoanji Temple in Kyoto was unforgettable. In the Garden of Meditation a few rocks of unusual shape, partly covered with fine moss, are widely and unevenly placed in a carefully raked courtyard of gravel, and the whole surrounded by a broad platform of weathered and worn wood. Sitting shoeless and cross-legged with other visitors who had stopped to meditate, the serenity and peace of the garden came to me almost as a physical experience. I began to feel the calmness and confidence and strength of being part of the created world of him who is the author of all strength and peace.

With delicate sensitivity and artistic skill the temple had been designed to communicate the beauty and serenity of God's creation. What a contrast it was to most of our chapels and churches, whose designs communicate very little, and the spoken word is the main element of communication. In that Kyoto experience I learned that through senses other than hearing, and through life processes other than thought one can experience "the Word without whom was not anything made that was made."

Can Christians learn from China?

In modern China, the people have sought the objectives of "salvation" in totally other ways. They have rejected religion, yet seem to have discovered by another route many of the ideals of community and meaning which are central to religions they rejected. Bronson P. Clark, executive secretary of the American Friends Service Committee, in late 1971 spent twenty-five days in China. Later, he wrote:

> I recently visited China after an absence of twenty-five years. It was an overwhelming experience to me to see the vast changes which have been made in that period. Enormous systems of flood control and water conservation have changed the landscape, the cities I knew are quite unrecognizable, and vast industrial complexes are springing up. . . . In 1945 and 1946, I witnessed cholera epidemics and saw evidence of the abysmal poverty of a desperate people who could not feed themselves adequately. On this recent visit my wife and I were aware of the comparative well-being of the population. . . . China's revolution embodies some great principles, from which we in the west could learn with profit.[3]

And then he lists eleven achievements he saw as "contributions which, if adapted to our own cultural and social situation, could represent significant developments in solving some difficult dilemmas facing our society." His list includes:

1) the involvement of everyone, particularly youth
2) the idea of service for love and not for profit
3) the absence of corruption
4) China's attention to conservation and ecology
5) the decision-making process now employed in China
6) the development of health services and family planning
7) care for offenders and the mentally ill
8) the fact that time seems well-balanced between academic study and actual physical involvement in work
9) organizational methods
10) problem solving taking place at all levels
11) the inner poise and self-confidence of the Chinese.

Such observations about life in China might be dismissed as the sentimental enthusiasm of a visitor taken in by skillful Chinese propaganda. But they come from a man of recognized knowledge and judgment in international affairs, who had the added perspective of service in China before the People's Republic was set up. And many other competent observers have given similar reports.

Clark points out that the best-known slogan in all of the People's Republic, "Serve the people," is indispensable as the driving idea of the Cultural Revolution. In the little red book of *Quotations from Chairman Mao,* the chapter "Serving the People" draws a lesson from the life of Norman Bethune, the Canadian doctor who gave his life working for the Red Army.

We must all learn the spirit of absolute selflessness from him [Bethune]. With this spirit everyone can be very useful to the people. A man's ability may be great or small, but if he has this spirit, he is already noble-minded and pure, a man of moral integrity and above vulgar interests, a man who is of value to the people.[4]

How strange that a society that has rejected Christianity seems to express many of the ideals of service, community involvement and compassion for the needy which Christianity preaches but often fails to practice. It is also remarkable that a Quaker should see in the people of China an inner quietness and confidence, which stand in sharp contrast to the restlessness of our society.

As we encounter people of other faiths and ideologies, and as we experience something of their insights and values, what position are we to take in relation to them? Shall we regard them as enemies, competitors or allies? Shall we simply ignore them? Or rather shall we see them as part of our one human family, sharing with us the need of a salvation we cannot achieve for ourselves.

Dialogue: inevitable, urgent, promising

In such a time of encounter we must show initiative and boldness in exploring ways forward to community and communication. That exploration has begun, through experiments in dialogue.

A Canadian study group defined dialogue as "a ruthlessly honest sharing of our understanding of the fundamental issues of human life, with someone who does not share our understanding of Christ as Savior and Lord. It means on the one hand, a willingness to lay all we believe and are on the line, and on the other hand, it involves listening with everything in us to what he has to say." [5] Experience has shown such dialogue is not easy. It has hazards as well as hopes.

[Dialogue] is inevitable because everywhere in the world Christians are now living in a pluralistic society.

—International Review of Mission

In recent years, a number of organized dialogues have taken place through the initiative of various departments of the World Council of Churches. Some have been between people of two faiths, and some between people of several faiths. And during the past ten years, institutes for encounter with other faiths have been set up in various parts of the world. Perhaps best known of these are the Christian Institute for the Study of Religion and Society at Bangalore, in India, and Tao Fang Shan, the Christian monastery in Hong Kong.

Most recently, these centers have focused on the task of dialogue with those who represent the actual expressions of their faith today. The modern form of most faiths has been profoundly influenced by science and Western thought, and is very different from classical scriptures and teachings.

An important attempt at multi-religious dialogue took place in March 1970 when persons from many of these centers met together in Lebanon. The group, which included Hindus, Buddhists, Christians and Moslems, addressed itself to the theme "Dialogue Between Men of Living Faiths—Present Discussions and Future Possibilities."

From that meeting, it was evident to the Christians that before they could converse usefully with men of other faiths, they needed a profound reexamination of their own faith to clarify their basic stance in relation to other faiths. To this end, a consultation of Christian theologians met in Zurich two months later, and from that meeting came an important paper, reproduced in the *International Review of Mission* of October 1970. Among other things it said:

All the circumstances of human life on the globe at this present stage force upon us the search for a world community in which men can share and act together.

Dialogue between Christians and men of other commitments . . . is an inevitable, urgent and promising manner of discovering how to bring together God's offer of communion in Christ and our diverse ways of common human living. . . .

[Dialogue] is *inevitable* because everywhere in the world Christians are now living in a pluralistic society.

It is *urgent* because all men are under common pressures in the search for justice, peace and a hopeful future and all are faced with the challenge to live together as human beings.

It is *full of opportunity* because Christians can now, as never before, discover the meaning of the Lordship of Christ and the implications for the mission of the Church in a truly universal context of common living and common urgency.

Men, whether Christian or not, must live together and do live together. Dialogues, designed to get to the deepest levels of commitment and directed to the most serious explorations of common action are, therefore, a clear human demand at this hour of human history.[6]

The importance of dialogue was recognized at the world level when the World Council of Churches' Central Committee, meeting in Addis Ababa in January 1971, gave its major study time to this issue. Considerable debate was sparked by a controversial paper by George Khodr of the

Orthodox Church, "Christianity in a Pluralistic World—The Work of the Holy Spirit."

In this paper he pointed out the double dangers of non-dialogue. First, there is the danger of increasing divisiveness in the human race at a time when man is seeking unity. And second, there is the danger of all religions being put into a melting pot and ending up as some sort of "lowest common denominator" religion.

Many people fear dialogue because they fear that any openness to those of other faiths will somehow weaken their own faith. We need to recognize that this is precisely one of the dangers of non-dialogue. If we do not seek to understand the essential elements of our own faith, and to hear what are the essential elements of the faith of the other man, we are in greater danger of ending up by default with a religion which is nothing but a mixture of our mutual confusions.

What is the Christian stance in a day of universal faiths?

As we try to understand the relation of Christianity to other faiths, we must not forget that we in the West have often equated world history solely with Mediterranean and European history. We have seen other nations as being on the periphery of world history, as agents on whom we acted rather than as full participants in world history themselves. Khodr states:

The Church has taken up the sociological shape of Christian nations. The Christian world in the West as well as in the East was identified with the dwelling place of peace, of light and of knowledge. The world of the non-christians was that of war and darkness. . . . Infidels, heretics and schismatics have to be brought into the church through missionary activity, through proselytism, or through cultural colonialism when persecution and war become unacceptable, so that there will only be "one flock and one shepherd." The Established Institutional Church thus becomes the centre of the world. . . . The rest of the world should come into . . . the Church through a salvation which is based on the universal extension of the Christian way of life founded on the authority of the West.[7]

Such an attitude may have been credible and tenable in a day when every part of the world was dominated by the West, when most other religions were still identified with particular cultures and regions, when they had not yet considered themselves as faiths for all mankind, and when they had not yet set up any kind of world missionary activity.

Now, however, the violent and often offensive impact of the West has stirred the great faiths to proclaim in no uncertain terms that they are universal, and to declare that theirs is an inclusive, comprehensive faith as over against the "exclusivism" of Christianity. They also have become involved in world mission activities.

Speaking of the renewal and resurgence of other religions, all claiming to be universal faiths, Khodr stated:

The question remains as to whether Christianity is, in its nature, as exclusive of other religions as has been globally proclaimed up till now.

Faced with questions like these, the Christian community must now dig deeply into the Bible to rediscover its proper stance in relation to the claims of other living faiths, and to clarify how it can make a responsible witness in the new context.

Christian basis for dialogue

As we explore the Christian basis for witness to men of other faiths we should keep clearly in mind what our aim is: "to further the proclamation to the whole world of the gospel of Jesus Christ, to the end that all may believe in him and be saved." We are also helped by the affirmation of faith already quoted from "Salvation Today."

We believe that God has acted and still acts. Jesus the Saviour is the focus of God's saving acts, who brought the world salvation by his incarnation, life, death and resurrection. Through the Holy Spirit he is at work today, accomplishing God's purpose of salvation. Our task as Christians is to witness, through word and deed, to this work of Christ and his Spirit among us in today's world.[8]

It is when we believe we own the truth that we are afraid of dialogue, because we fear that our possession may be taken from us. When we understand that truth and salvation belong only to God, and that our task is only to witness to Christ, then we are freed for true dialogue and authentic witness. As we establish a more positive relationship with men of other faiths, we do so as a living out of our own faith and of our belief in the wholeness of creation. The Zurich Consultation said:

Dialogue between Christians and men of other living faiths, being understood within the context of God's mission to all men, stems from love and is seeking the fruit of love. True love never only gives. It is also concerned always to receive. For love is a relationship and a power of mutual respect. Love therefore is concerned always with the reality, the freedom and the fulfilment of the other.[9]

Some Christians fear that dialogue with men of other faiths is a betrayal of mission, that we should only proclaim and not listen. And some men of other faiths suspect that dialogue is simply a new tool for mission, an approach which has no serious intent to listen but only to proclaim.

Problems of this kind force us to look again at how we understand the presence of Christ outside organized Christianity. We believe that the mission of the church stems from and is a part of God's activity of salvation, which is particularly embodied in Christ. Because in Christ all things hold together, then people of other faiths are also in his hands. For Christ's sake we must take them seriously as part of what God is doing.

Love is a relationship and a power of mutual respect . . . concerned always with the reality, the freedom and the fulfilment of the other.

—International Review of Mission

At the same time we must be true to the task of letting them know about the Christ who gives us this understanding. Witnessing to the love of God in Christ is an obligation inherent in the gospel. Engaging in dialogue simply for the sake of mutual understanding loses its meaning unless we as Christians bear witness to the salvation we receive in Jesus Christ.

The adoption by the WCC Central Committee of its "Interim Policy Statement and Guidelines" on dialogue is an important event, for it represents a firm statement by a great representative Christian body of positive action in an area where other Christians have often failed by default. This statement includes the following affirmation:

Our faith in Jesus Christ who became a man for all men in all times sustains us in dialogue. The expression of this faith in the life and witness of the church leads us to develop relationships with men of different faiths and ideologies. Jesus Christ who makes us free draws us out of isolation into genuine dialogue into which we enter with faith in the promise of Jesus Christ that the Holy Spirit will lead us into all truth.[10]

The Roman Catholic Church had taken a somewhat more cautious initial step in Vatican II, the Ecumenical Council of 1963–65, in issuing a "Declaration on the Relationship of the Church to Non-Christian Religions." And in 1964 Pope Paul VI set up the Secretariat for Non-Christian Religions with aims: "to create a climate of cordiality between Christians and followers of other religions, to dissipate prejudice and ignorance especially among Catholics, and to establish fruitful contact with members of other religions concerning questions of common interest."[11] The emphasis has been on what men have in common, the solidarity of mankind, and the theme of "Christ, the light of the world."

God has no favorites

We discover in the biblical story that it was frequently through people and events outside the church that God spoke a new word.

This was not easy for the New Testament Christians to accept. In the tenth and eleventh chapters of Acts we have a vivid account of how Peter and then the church in Jerusalem were taught the lesson. God used Cornelius, a Roman centurion, to communicate with Peter. Cornelius was directed by an angel of God to invite Peter to his home. Peter was reluctant to go because, as he said, "a Jew is forbidden to visit or associate with a man of another race."

But through a vision God led him to go, and through that experience he heard a fresh word of Christ. He concluded, "I now see how true it is that God has no favourites, but that in every nation the man who is godfearing and does what is right is acceptable to him" (Acts 10:34–35). And through the openness to hear God's word through Cornelius, Peter made his witness. The outcome was that the Holy Spirit came on all who listened, and they were baptized.

Later in the book of Acts we have an account of Paul's witness in Athens at the Court of Areopagus. He said, "As I was going round looking at the objects of your worship, I noticed among other things an altar bearing the inscription 'To an Unknown God.' What you worship but do not know—this is what I now proclaim" (Acts 17:23). Paul gave their god a name. Christians are those who know the name of him who through his Spirit has been at work among men of every race and nation.

God is already there before us

How often the Christian missionary feels that Christ has preceded him. James Seunarine of the United Theological College of the West Indies, having just returned from studies in India, has said: "Christ does not come to India as a stranger; he comes into his own. Christ comes to India not from Europe, but directly from the Father." [12]

In my early days as a missionary in Manchuria, I remember talking to a small group of village people about the Christian faith. At the close an illiterate, but very wise old woman came up to me. "I am glad now to hear about this Jesus Christ and his ways," she said, "because I have always known it would be like this."

Donald V. Wade, professor of religions at the University of Toronto, has written:

Wherever you go and whatever you meet, God is already there before you. Christ's presence precedes yours. He always provides his forerunners. The whole world of reality is the realm of God's action and purpose. He is everywhere at work in history and there is no monopoly on his grace. Christian presence does not cause Christ's presence but witnesses to it. Our task is that of a kind of interpreting presence.[13]

Eight methods and conditions for dialogue

1. The first comment comes from the *IRM* article of October 1970.

Dialogue has to be carried out in the context of the pressures of secularization, and of the common quest for the future of man that history forces upon all of us. It should deal with both the quest for true interiority and personal fulfilment as well as with the struggle for a peaceful society with justice and dignity for all.[14]

All religion is being questioned, and all mankind is confronted with the great question of human destiny.

2. There will be a diversity of dialogues.

The churches find themselves within history in a diversity of situations. This diversity makes for a diversity of dialogues, defined not only by political, social and geographical circumstances, but by the diversity of partners. The dialogue with Hindus is different from that with Buddhists, with Muslims, with Jews, etc.—and different too from that with Marxists. Each Christian community involved in dialogue is thus in a particular situation and has a specific partner or partners.[15]

3. Dialogue should take place at world levels as well as local and regional. While each congregation may be involved in dialogue locally, it is also part of the universal church, and has a share in the calling of the whole church

to work for the unity of mankind. For this reason, the local congregation has a responsibility to support dialogue at the world level.

Among the first to recognize the Christ and bring their own particular gifts to the baby in the manger were men of other faiths; the Wise Men from the East.

---

4. The dialogue which is most effective may often be indirect, such as dialogue about common *secular* problems. James Seunarine has elaborated:

When Hindus and Muslims and Christians get together to study political realities, the realities of job situations, the question of housing, of food supply, and so on—it is then that the religious presuppositions which underlie our actions really come to the surface. And when we get together to tackle the real problems of humanity which bring suffering and degradation, which are a real challenge to our total resources, then we are likely to have understanding, to have real dialogue. It is when we take this approach, in some sort of fellowship together, that we are likely to find the presence of Christ with us.[16]

5. Dialogue must take place in freedom.

Each partner must be understood as he understands himself, and his freedom to be committed to his faith must be fully respected. Without this freedom to be committed, to be open, to witness, to change *and to be changed,* dialogue is impossible.[17]

6. Real dialogue cannot avoid conflict. Because real dialogue arises out of living faiths, it cannot escape places of conflict—nor should it try to do so—for the sake of false harmony. The fear of conflict has often cut off the Christian community from the kind of living relationships with the non-Christian environment through which alone it can witness to the Christ.

7. Dialogue involves more than just verbal communication. "We may discover each other in significant silence, in the experience of living together, in the experiences of sharing some aspects of our devotion. Respectful attendance at and participation in one another's worship may thus open up new levels of communication and dialogue." [18]

However, in this very important area of devotion and worship it is often difficult to draw the line between helpful sharing and sentimental common worship which is only contradictory and confusing. In certain circumstances, worship organized and conducted by different faiths together may hinder the cause of true dialogue. But, at the same time, our dialogue will be impoverished if we are not open to the worship dimension of each other's life.

8. We enter into dialogue with the joyous expectation of learning more of Christ. Because we believe that he is universal and unique we cannot state that our particular way of understanding and worshiping him is absolute and complete. An Indian Christian, Raymond Panikkar, has pointed out that what we know as Christianity is only one of many possible forms of expressing faith in Christ. It is conditioned by the philosophical and sociological forms of our Western world. Through dialogue with those of other faiths we may break out of traditions which obscure the Christ, and may see him in his full radiance.

Our confidence is in the Christ

We go into dialogue with the belief that the Holy Spirit leads men to the Christ. We see dialogue as a journey of exploration in which we discover more of the nature and fullness of the Christ, and in which the other person hears of the One for whom kings and prophets of every age and race have waited.

Donald Wade has said:

> What is there in the great religious traditions that can't emerge in the many-splendored creations of the love of God? Let us not be too precipitate in thinking of conversion as simply the defeat of the other. That's not the way of Christ. There are great treasures of wisdom and insight and feeling and experience that can only be brought into Christ and be given their rightful place in the Kingdom.[19]

We should never forget that among the first to recognize the Christ and bring their own particular gifts to the baby in the manger were men of other faiths; the Wise Men from the East. Was it from their own wisdom or from the action of God's Spirit that they recognized the Star and followed it, and so were led to the Christ?

In spite of all their learning and all their enlarging experience, men still ask, "Where is he?"

5

"let my people go"

God's salvation includes liberation.
His people are to release captives.
The time for liberation is here!

Liberation of the oppressed and the fulfillment of human life is a theme which runs like a thread through the whole of biblical Good News as an integral element of God's purpose of salvation.

In Isaiah we find a marvelous vision of God's purpose for human society, where work shall come to glad fruition and every man shall have a place to live.

For behold, I create
new heavens and a new earth.
Former things shall no more be remembered
nor shall they be called to mind.

. . . . .

Men shall build houses and live to inhabit them,
plant vineyards and eat their fruit;
they shall not build for others to inhabit
not plant for others to eat.

My people shall live the long life of a tree,
and my chosen shall enjoy the fruit of their labor.
They shall not toil in vain or raise children for
misfortune.

—Isaiah 65:17, 21–23a

The glorious theme of the Magnificat, Mary's hymn of joy, is God's salvation for the oppressed and poor.

The deeds his own right arm has done
disclose his might:
the arrogant of heart and mind he has put to rout,
he has brought down monarchs from their thrones,
but the humble have been lifted high.
The hungry he has satisfied with good things,
the rich sent empty away.

—Luke 1:51–53

When Jesus announced his mission in Nazareth, he chose liberation as his theme, using the words of Isaiah.

The spirit of the Lord is upon me because he has
anointed me;
he has sent me to announce good news to the poor,
to proclaim release for prisoners and recovery of sight
for the blind;
to let the broken victims go free,
to proclaim the year of the Lord's favor.

—Luke 4:18–19

Our world: the pampered and the plundered

In sharp contrast with these glorious biblical visions of liberation are the realities of the present world. The vast inequalities between the "haves" and "have nots" are clearly visible. But our affluence and freedom in Europe and North America have blinded us to the poverty and enslavement experienced by the great majority of the world's people.

Today, rapidity of transportation and communication has made the world one. We can remain blind no longer. We know that while we dwell in security and enjoy the fruits of our labors, for most of the world the marvelous vision of Isaiah has not happened and is not happening, and indeed may *never* happen, if present trends persist. While we believe that the outcome of life is in God's hands, to be achieved in his good time, we cannot allow this confidence to relieve us from what is in our power to do.

Garth Legge, a secretary of the Division of World Outreach of the United Church of Canada and a sensitive expert on development in Latin America and Africa, has vividly described the problem.

> We have in the world disparities of such fundamental quality that the vision of Isaiah could never be realized except maybe for a few of us, unless we give forceful attention to that reality. We live in a world of the pampered and the plundered, not just the rich and the poor. We are pampered. And the other people out there—they are the plundered. The systemic violence institutionalized in the world today means that they are being plundered every day they draw breath. And we are on their backs. And what is happening to the world as I see it? The rage of God's common people is building. That's the only word I can use for it—the rage of God's common people is building.[1]

Human nature calls for justice

Within the human family there is a deeply rooted sense of human rights. It seems an inborn part of human nature. When my children were small they were as content with a small candy as with a large one—just so long as brother or sister did not have a larger one. They were ready to take a reasonable part in dishwashing and other jobs about the house—just so long as they were not asked to carry a larger share than their brothers or sisters. As soon as an inequality of things received or work demanded arose, so did tension and conflict.

It is not poverty that hurts, but poverty in the midst of affluence. It is not restriction that hurts, but restriction in the midst of freedom. People want to have their rightful share in the goods and privileges of the whole human race. This expectation of justice which will free men from whatever oppressions keep them from being fully human, poses a deep and inescapable challenge to all Christians.

It is those who make peaceful revolution impossible who will make violent revolution inevitable.

—John F. Kennedy

Both the victims and the victimizers are oppressed. Both need liberation to become new men. This is not simply a *liberation from* oppression, but a *liberation into* rightful participation with the rest of mankind in the life of all humanity. People desire to live in responsible relationship with their neighbors and not have all their strength absorbed merely in the effort to stay alive.

The time of the just and the human is at hand

The revolt against the centuries-old domination by Europe and North America is seen particularly in the Caribbean. The "new Caribbean man" now wants a real part in the decisions which determine his own life, and is resolved to become master in his own house. For too long, decisions which vitally affected his life were made in Britain for the benefit of the British, or in North America for the benefit of North Americans. Idris Hamid of Trinidad, a dedicated pastor and theologian, has written:

> God is calling us to take responsibility for our future. Our past has been a defuturised past. Hopelessness reigned. We were the ploy of other peoples' future. . . . Our lives and communities were ordered to benefit and stabilise the future of others. While they gained a future, we lost ours. Not only were we robbed of our future, we were robbed of our past. . . . Our rich cultural heritages were labelled as uncivilised. In our schools we were further inflicted with a denigration of our past. In our religious training one is hard put to find any attempt to see God operating in our former cultures and in our Caribbean history.[2]

In his penetrating analysis he points out how the false dichotomy between body and spirit allowed us to send and support priests and missionaries to save souls, and at the same time benefit economically from the exploitation of the bodies of the Caribbean people.

> We were encouraged to endure our suffering, to be patient, to lay hold on future rewards in the sweet by and by. We were drilled into the virtues of poverty and patience. The evils of riches were held before us. . . . Some of our emerging leaders are beginning to see through this and are calling for a new theology; a new religious base for our development. . . . [They ask,] Is there no word from the Lord? . . . As a people—a Caribbean people—is there no word from the Lord for us people with our common historical experience?[3]

That same pressing desire for liberation is found also among black victims of white oppression in many parts of southern Africa. I saw something of this firsthand in a recent visit to Kenya, Malawi and Zambia, each of which has its quota of political refugees from adjacent African countries. The magnitude and complexity of the problem in southern Africa and the urgent need for solution is described in a report prepared for the All Africa Conference of Churches, which states that there are more than thirty million who have almost literally no part in their own government. Many have been living as exiles from their own countries for almost a generation.

It is evident that the time for liberation is here. All across the world voices are crying out for freedom in a unified way never seen before. This longed-for freedom is celebrated by Roberto Padilla, who during the Cuban revolution wrote:

> Life has come out into the open!
> People are on the roads again,
> Rejoicing.
> He who bled but yesterday,
> Today is singing.
>
> Oh, dreamer of bitter nights,
> Eyes hooded with suspicion
> And with terror,
> Break out of your trance.
> For the love of your people,
> Awake!
> The time of the just and the human is at hand.[4]

Liberation: central to mission

Throughout Latin America, where dictatorships and oligarchies predominate, a tremendous movement toward liberation has become the central concern of the churches.

In the light of Christian faith and in the context of Latin American problems, they see the goal of liberation as containing at least three elements: (1) the political liberation of oppressed peoples and social classes; (2) the liberation and fulfillment of mankind in the course of history; and (3) liberation from sin as a condition of life into communion of all men with God—especially including the liberation of the rich, by making them realize the state of sin in which they live while they unjustly exclude the poor from a fair share of human living.

The necessity that mission lays upon us to commit ourselves in the struggle for liberation has been vividly expressed by Bishop Antonio Fragoso of Brazil:

> Christ did not come only to liberate man from sin. He came to liberate him from the consequence of sin. These consequences are in our houses, in our streets, in our cities, and inside ourselves, too. They take various forms: prostitution; racial discrimination; marginalization of peasants; lack of roads, of housing, and of sanitary facilities; concentration of economic power in the hands of a few; hoarding of land by a few, while the great majority have no land to work; the availability of bank credits to only one group. . . . Christ sought man's liberation, his global liberation. That was the meaning of his mission: He was the Liberator. That is why all Christians who adhere to Christ and want to follow Him are called upon, by what is most profound in our mission, to commit themselves in the struggle for the global liberation of men.[5]

This kind of understanding raises sharply the question as to whether there can be any mission without liberation. Is there not an inextricable relationship between these two concepts? Perhaps mission *necessitates* liberation.

While it is true that freedom in Christ is freedom in the midst of oppression as well as freedom from oppression, nevertheless the issue is freedom. Liberation is thus both spiritual and physical. Both are equally part of God's salvation. In no way can we limit the concept of salvation to a kind of spiritual transformation which ignores real physical oppression. Neither can we direct our efforts toward political liberation without at the same time working toward that liberation of spirit which flows from moral cleansing and personal renewal through the forgiveness of Christ.

This point has been made with rare clarity by Canon Douglas Webster in the Annual Sermon for 1972 of the Church Mission Society in England:

In the Bible God began to show what he meant by salvation when he rescued slaves from Egypt and promised them a land flowing with milk and honey. Christian salvation is not less than that but more. There must be a concrete deliverance from whatever bondage defaces and dehumanizes mankind today. . . . That is why the true proclaimer of salvation, the true evangelist, will always be on the side of the deprived, not necessarily in sharing their opinions but in sensitivity to their plight. Evangelism in these terms means agitation. . . . The full-blooded salvation of the Bible does not by-pass economic and political realities.[6]

In his book *A Faith for This One World?* Lesslie Newbigin speaks of "loving service to the world" as the proper mark of the new community, the church.

Just as the presence of the Spirit in Jesus meant that healing power flowed from him, so the presence of the same Spirit in the Church will issue in all kinds of loving service to men according to their need. The Church is to be the servant of men. This is not a matter of conscious missionary strategy, though it is part of the Church's total mission. It is simply a matter of being what God created a human being to be. To put it bluntly, if you meet a man in need, and if you are in a position to meet his need, if you are a man in whom the Spirit of God dwells, you will do what the situation requires and there will be no more nonsense about it.[7]

The obligation which the gospel lays upon the church to espouse justice even in the midst of controversial situations led the 1972 General Assembly of the United Presbyterian Church in the U.S.A. to prepare and adopt a statement on the rationale for the prophetic role. It declared:

> The first and continuous obligation of the church is to be accountable to the call of the Gospel. The church is for reconciliation, for justice, for "Shalom," for others. Because the church knows this mission, it must exert moral pressure for the transformation of society.[8]

It is often through concern for political liberation that people are led into the total liberation of Christ. On a recent visit to one of the Third World countries where a black majority is being oppressed by a white minority, Garth Legge preached on the Magnificat: "The deeds his own right arm has done disclose his might: the arrogant of heart and mind he has put to rout, he has brought down monarchs from their thrones, but the humble have been lifted high." Later, in speaking of his experience, he said, "You could just feel the feedback. This was the word of God to them—it wasn't *my* word. It had political overtones, and they were inescapable. But they got the message. Am I wrong in thinking that Christ the Liberator was communicated in that way?" [9]

Teaching men to live in justice and peace

Early in 1972 the World Council of Churches (WCC) and the All Africa Conference of Churches (AACC) made a great witness for Christ in Africa in facilitating the negotiation of peaceful settlement of the sixteen-year war in south Sudan. The WCC and AACC had been involved since 1965 in efforts toward reconciliation, taking an active role as go-betweens and advisors for the protagonists. The Emperor of Ethiopia had acted as intermediary for the talks.

When a copy of the agreement was given to the Emperor on behalf of the WCC by Canon Burgess Carr (general secretary of the AACC) who had acted as moderator of the peace negotiations, the Emperor said:

> We are very grateful for the part the World Council of Churches and the All Africa Conference of Churches has [*sic*] played in bringing the two brothers together. As instruments of God, you have carried out His Will for peace and justice. You were able to bring two brothers together again. What joy is there more than this? What you have done is of lasting value. This, you managed to do in accordance with the dictates of our Creator, who said to you, the leaders of His church: Go and teach men to live in peace, in justice and in brotherhood. And you have carried out the Will of the Lord. You would not have succeeded in your deliberations if the blessing and goodwill of God did not prevail in the meeting. May God bless this agreement and its execution for the interest of all the people of the Sudan.[10]

The dimension of justice and its achievement

Legge has said, "Unless everything we do today is somehow informed by the awareness of the dimension of justice, we are failing Christus Liberator. For if mission is liberation in Christ, then we must seek justice for our neighbor."

This leads us to the very difficult question of how justice is to be achieved. And this in turn forces us to face the problem of violence. If those now in power in oppressive regimes in many parts of the world are determined to hold that power—and they do so by tightly imposed violence—it seems impossible that liberation can come without revolution.

In a 1972 meeting, Cynthia Wedel, then president of the National Council of the Churches of Christ in the USA, urged her hearers not to get "up-tight" about the word

I took off my cassock
to be more truly a priest.

—Camilo Torres

revolution. "Fearmongers," she said, "like to imply that revolution has to be violent, but revolution actually is just another word for change. . . . God is the author of the revolution of our day. The trouble comes not from those seeking change but from the entrenched and the privileged who fear any change. It seems pretty obvious that God has now decided that the time has come for all people to share in the riches of the good earth," said Mrs. Wedel. [But when those entrenched] "refuse, often with contempt and disdain, to listen to the cries for help from the oppressed, they force the oppressed to take direct action." [11]

The question of violence is a profound concern of all revolutionary movements, but particularly those in the nations of Africa and Latin America. Legge has said:

> Much of the violence we see today is counterviolence. It is imposed by the system, which oppresses, dehumanizes and plunders people. John Kennedy said that it is those who make peaceful revolution impossible who will make violent revolution inevitable.

How can we condemn liberation movements which are driven to violence as a last resort, if we do not first condemn the regimes which are withholding human rights from multitudes, holding them in bondage by daily threat of terror, violence and death? Can we raise a great outcry against patriotic fighters who attack where they can and sometimes endanger the innocent, if we do not first protest the institutionalized violence of armies, navies and air forces which terrorize, maim and kill thousands of innocent civilians?

Dom Helder Câmara of Brazil has written:

Violence number one, mother of all violence, is born from injustices. Thus the young people who want to interpret the violence to the oppressed, react against violence number one with violence number two. And this one provokes violence number three, the fascist violence. I don't accept any of these three violences, but I can understand violence number two. I detest the one who is passive, who is quiet, and I love the one who dares, who struggles.[12]

Fergus Kerr has written in *Frontier Magazine* recently:

Where some existing social order contains as much injustice now as could ever arise if that order were overthrown, it becomes possible to think that a revolution to bring justice and freedom to the least of the brethren could be supported and encouraged in the name of the gospel of love. The time may have come when the Church must take the side of revolutions because they are just.[13]

Camilo Torres, a priest of Colombia, died fighting as a guerrilla. Before he was killed, he explained that this was the only way left to him to exercise his priesthood in Christ on behalf of his oppressed brethren. He protested that people should not waste time discussing whether the soul is immortal, when they know that hunger is definitely mortal. "I took off my cassock," he said, "to be more truly a priest."

Confrontation as a way of witness

We are aware now of the existence of political oppression in our world, and our consciences are becoming sensitized to it. But we Christians are often ineffective in situations of conflict because of the oppression of the long established religious tradition of avoiding social or political conflict. We need to study again the ways in which men of the Bible and particularly Jesus Christ expressed themselves as agents of reconciliation in the midst of unjust situations.

It is difficult to wage a revolution without the Bible. It is even more difficult not to bring about a revolution with the Bible.

Some of our Lord's greatest problems were with the religious establishment. He seemed almost to invite confrontation and conflict—particularly with those religious leaders who were concerned more in binding men with the law than setting them free with the truth. On many occasions Jesus could have avoided provocation. But he healed the man on the Sabbath rather than waiting until the next day. In Jericho he sought the friendship of Zacchaeus, the despised tax collector. He was often seen eating and drinking with publicans and sinners.

His whole ministry was filled with confrontation and conflict. As early as the second chapter of Mark's record we read of a series of intentional confrontations with the lawyers and the Pharisees, and the beginning of their plotting to kill him. In his home town the people heard him first with admiration but he chose a message which so infuriated them they took him to the brow of the hill to hurl him off.

Robert Raines, co-minister of the First Methodist Church in Germantown, Philadelphia, has observed that many young people are taking a new look at Jesus and finding the strong Jesus of the Gospel records. He reports:

They are taking the wraps off a gentle Jesus meek and mild, smelling flowers or carrying lambs, to discover a tough young man who associated with the poor and outcasts of his day, flayed the religious establishment for its hypocrisy and injustice, broke sacred religious laws again and again in order to serve human need, and put on a smashing one-man demonstration in the most influential cathedral of the nation to protest its exploitation of the faithful.[14]

In a world of violence, peacemaking may be a very controversial issue. When issues of this sort were disturbing the 1972 Quadrennial General Conference of The United Methodist Church in the U.S.A., one of the Conference preachers reminded the delegates that though the church, like Jesus, may be labeled a troublemaker, it is really a peacemaker.

The peace of Jesus is not the calm of inactivity or the quietness of a stagnant pool; the stillness of submission to slavery or the death of the spirit by fear and oppression; the stalemate of conflicting forces or retreat into one's self. . . . Peacemakers in a cruciform world are viewed as troublemakers.[15]

We should not forget that many of the people Jesus gathered about him as followers were on the fringe of the religious establishment of his day, or even totally outside it and despised by it. We should not then be surprised if he chooses people and movements on the fringe of the organized church and of organized mission to spearhead some of the important forms of his mission today. The Holy Spirit is free and will move as it will.

One cannot read church history without discovering that many of the most effective and impressive forms of mission—including the world missionary movement—started on the fringe of the church establishment and as such have usually been distrusted and called heretical at their inception. While we do not despair of the institutional forms of church and mission, we must be willing to admit that they can develop structures and traditions which stifle the free expression of the Spirit.

Local congregation: sign or countersign?

And so we must examine our own church programs and structures. There is no way that we can stand as the "saving community" if we are insensitive to the real needs of real men in the real situations of history. The full-blooded salvation which God intends for all mankind will not be known across the world unless the church can free itself from traditional structures and programs which are too narrow for the service of the Lord and Savior of all mankind.

A sensitive pastor of the Guyana Presbyterian Church, Haimdat Sawh, has said:

> It seems to me that unless the church in the first place can understand its own nature and mission, unless it can free itself from the crippling self-preoccupation with which it is presently afflicted, unless it can liberate itself from the hardening of the institutional arteries, then it cannot exorcise the demands of hate and fear, exploitation, insensitivity.

He has confessed his own sense of failure in regard to the congregation where he serves.

> As I ask myself what has my particular congregation done for mission in the area in which I live, I must say, very little. Right across from the church where I serve is a whole sea of

squatters, people who are refugees from their own country. These people had to flee for their lives from areas of unrest, and hastily tried to set up houses and live in this new area. You can imagine the overcrowding, the substandard housing and all that goes with it—the lack of sanitary facilities and even pure water.

And the church right across the road there? It's not a wealthy church. It doesn't have plenty of property. Yet it seems to me that the church there is completely unaware of the existence of this need at its very doorstep.

When this happens, I think that the church, rather than being the instrument of God's action, is becoming the countersign. Instead of witnessing to God's activity in the world and joining in that activity, it is actually engaging in an act of opposition.

But I want to say that if God cannot bring the kingdom through the church, he'll bring it in spite of the church. Just as God abandoned the old Israel in favor of the new, so he can abandon the church and raise an instrument meet for his purpose, in Guyana, in Trinidad, in the world.

However it seems to me it has pleased God that the church is the instrument—imperfect, inadequate, capable of all sorts of criticism being directed at it—but it is the instrument God has chosen. And we are the people who right now are the instruments of his purpose. The question is, are we going to allow God to fulfill that purpose through us? [16]

6

toward the fully human

Development is equal opportunity for each to develop in full dignity and rights as a human being, to life in all its fulness.

Is there anything like God here?

I look for a God of this world. . . . I look for God, or for the power of God, or for the men of God, to do something about the poverty and oppression and the crime in the world. When I do not see an end to these things, when I see them continuing and getting worse, I ask, where is God?

I ask, is God not of this world, is God a God of the Bible and of the dead, or God of the rich and not of the poor, and in some parts, God of the white and not of the black? . . .

It is easy to say believe—quite easy. But when you are here, living next door to hooligans and prostitutes, when the girl next door is raped and the boy next door is charged for robbery and the woman next door commits suicide, you know that God is not here, that he was never here.

Look at the amount of churches in Port-of-Spain! Look at the amount of masses that are sung, and the amount of gospels read! But look at this city and ask, really ask yourself if there is anything or anyone like God in it, and you must answer no, there is no God here. If he was here, he has left. And I hear it is so all over the world.[1]

These are the bitter words of Caribbean novelist E. Lovelace as quoted by Idris Hamid, a minister of the Presbyterian Church of Trinidad and Grenada, in *In Search of New Perspectives,* a paper commissioned for the 1971 Caribbean Ecumenical Consultation for Development.

Hamid goes on to say:

> God has a concern for the concrete conditions of our existence. Down in Pharaoh's Egypt there was no talk of "spiritualised" freedom. It was concrete political emancipation and when bargaining failed, God walked off the bargaining table and set his people free! . . . [Therefore] when God becomes identified with man in the life of Jesus, he befriends the poor, the sick, the ordinary, the outcasts. And to enter His Kingdom everyone must identify with and minister to the imprisoned, the naked, the sick, the hungry (Matthew 25:31–46)—and we may add, the unemployed, the brutalized, the dehumanised.[2]

In a deeply moving address to a world gathering on development, Dom Helder Câmara outlined vividly some of the realities of the present situation of mankind.

> It is a sad fact that . . . 80 percent of the world's resources are at the disposal of 20 percent of the world's inhabitants. While one segment of humanity is rich and growing richer, the rest will struggle in varying degrees and have little certainty of breaking out of their stagnation in the next decades.
>
> Our responsibility as Christians makes us tremble. The Northern hemisphere, the developed area of the world, the 20 percent who possess 80 percent of the world's resources, are of Christian origin. What impression can our African and Asian brethren and the masses in Latin America have of Christianity, if the tree is to be judged by its fruits? For we Christians are largely responsible for the unjust world in which we live.

Christianity is invoked in order to lead a sort of crusade against Communism. Christianity is invoked in order to combat the wave of hatred, deep-rooted resentment and terror which is rising everywhere.

The 20 percent who let 80 percent stagnate in a situation which is often sub-human—what right have they to allege that Communism crushes the human person? The 20 percent who are keeping the 80 percent in a situation which is often sub-human—are they or are they not responsible for the violence and hatred which are beginning to break out all over the world? [3]

We are told today that if all the hungry people in the world were to stand one and one-half feet apart in single file, the line would stretch around the world twenty times. By the year 2000, unless something radically changes in the food distribution patterns, the line will go around the world forty times. And the computers indicate that in the United States alone—in that "affluent" nation—the line would stretch six thousand miles.

In *The Wretched of the Earth,* Frantz Fanon of Algeria has written:

This European opulence is literally scandalous, for it has been founded on slavery, it has been nourished with the blood of slaves and it comes directly from the soil and from the sub-soil of that under-developed world. The well-being and the progress of Europe have been built up with the sweat and the dead bodies of Negroes, Arabs, Indians and the yellow races. We have decided not to overlook this any longer.[4]

Historically it is a fact that the nations of the West grew rich on the spoils of empire: Britain from India, Africa and the Caribbean; France from Africa and Southeast Asia; Holland from Indonesia; Belgium from the Congo; Portugal and Spain from the Caribbean, South America and Africa;

and the United States from growing access to all these areas. While not denying benefits from the colonial period, the basic fact remains that economic arrangements were set up primarily for the benefit of the metropolitan powers. They grew affluent while the colonial countries remained poor.

At a 1968 church conference on world development, the distinguished economist Barbara Ward Jackson highlighted the facts of inequality with some shocking statistics and a damning conclusion.

> The annual increase in Atlantic income is greater than the total income of Africa and the Indian subcontinent. The United States is twelve times wealthier than all its "sister republics" in Latin America put together. Expenditure on alcohol and tobacco alone in the North Atlantic countries is more than double the entire national income of India. These are disproportions that are greater than the old chasm between rich and poor within traditional societies. Like a whole caravan of outsize camels, each loaded down with precious merchandise, the developed states lurch across the world—and there is not a needle's eye through which they can pass.[5]

In the face of these facts, Christians cannot be content with a piety which ignores the loud crying for social and economic justice. They would indeed be the "good cannibals" parodied in Gloria Maxson's little poem, *Warlords:*

> They still
> with lofty phrase
> ferocity define—
> good cannibals say grace before
> they dine.[6]

The gap between the rich and the poor is widening

The development problem is extremely complex. Statistics show that the rich nations are getting richer and the poor nations poorer, and the poor are increasing at three times the rate of the rich. Harold Sitahal, a Trinidadian pastor, has said: "Some make hasty judgments on the people concerned. The general tendency is for the rich to see their good fortune as a result of their own remarkable efforts and the destitution of the poor as the outcome of their lack of perseverance, nay more of their 'irresponsibility and moral decay.' "[7]

It is easier for a camel to go through the eye of a needle than for a rich man to enter the kingdom of God.

—Luke 18:25

But, he says, our present technological and economic structures are such that the rich are getting richer *at the expense of the poor,* and there is no way, apart from the most radical revolutionary change in the structure of society, for the poor nations to overtake the rich.

It has become apparent to many in the Third World that the political independence they gained within the last twenty-five years has not really solved their problems. In many cases, economic power is still in the hands of the former governing countries.

Sitahal has documented this:

When the individual undeveloped nations seek their unconditional independence they are faced with the withdrawal of colonial capital and technicians and the establishment of economic blockades by the powerful ex-colonial overlords. Those nations which compromise with the colonial powers find themselves in no better position than before. The former dominated country becomes an economically dependent country. The former colonial power makes occasional gestures of aid to the independent nations, but ensures that the former economic channels are intact. . . . Any socio-economic situation which is built upon the division of the human race into privileged and less privileged, or bestows untold power to a few over the many, must be challenged, as a distortion of the human situation.

Fanon says, "The question which is looming on the horizon is the need for a re-distribution of wealth. Humanity must reply to this question, or be shaken to pieces by it." [8]

The economies of the West are so vigorous that they dominate not only their own societies but also the societies of nations that are struggling to come to life economically. The question here is: Is that power being used for the prosperous, or for the poor? And there is a growing suspicion in our world that this economic power is *not* for the sake of the poor.

Where an economy dealing with a poor nation is in fact for the sake of the prosperous, there is a moral issue to be faced. The reason that a number of churches in the United States have been challenging large American corporations dealing with white racist governments in Angola and South Africa is because they feel that these corporations have not faced this issue.

There is no nation south of the Sahara in Africa with the gross national product of General Motors. Ranked alongside the nations of the world, General Motors stands sixteenth in Gross National Product, and Ford Motor Company is twenty-sixth. The economic power these corporations have is neither good nor bad. But how it is used is a profound biblical issue which Christians must confront.

A widening gap makes disaster inevitable

It is becoming increasingly evident that there is no possibility of world stability while the vast gap remains and widens between the affluent and the poor nations. These mounting inequalities are causing economic, political and military tensions which will explode with unprecedented violence unless steps are undertaken to correct them.

In Robert McNamara's analysis of civil disturbance, upheavals of government, and violence of all kinds in the one hundred twenty poor nations of the world, he has discerned a direct relationship between poverty and civil disturbance patterns. Hunger leads inevitably to disturbance.

Lester Pearson in a recent report to the United Nations has said that no world, any more than a nation, can live half full and half hungry without disaster. And Robert McNamara has suggested that the present direction of the world is in the direction of that disaster.

At a Montreal Conference of SODEPAX (the Catholic/Protestant world organization for Society, Development and Peace), two alternatives were offered:

> The first is to attempt to contain [the mounting] pressures by the oppressive use of power in order to preserve the present distribution of economic and political resources. The second is for Christians to join with all men who are struggling for a more just society to begin now to fashion a more just and humane world community, which includes the maximum feasible participation of all its members in decisions made for that community. For Christians, only the second alternative is possible.[9]

God's salvation concerns the needs of men now

A recurring and insistent theme of biblical faith is that hunger and suffering, pain and oppression shall be done away and men shall enter into freedom and fullness of life. The glory of biblical faith is that salvation relates to the development of men now as a part of that total life of Christ which even death does not terminate.

But the church has often taken the power out of these words by spiritualizing them and relating them only to life after death. When this happens the message of the church loses its power. It falls on deaf ears because vast multitudes across the world are crying out for someone to meet their present need. When their present need is not met they find it difficult to believe that God is concerned about them in any way. When the church does not have and express a passionate concern for the present needs of men everywhere, it may in effect become an obstacle rather than an instrument of the gospel.

For the Christian, says Lesslie Newbigin, compassionate action and evangelism can never be separated; neither should they be wrongly related.

> In particular, service must not be subordinated to evangelism. The Christian works of love should be as Christ's were, a spontaneous outflowing of the love of God for men, not a means to something else. . . . Preaching which is divorced from deeds of love is without power to evoke belief. Deeds of love which are permanently disconnected from witness to Christ evoke belief in the wrong thing. . . . In Christ's own ministry both the preaching of the good news and the manifold works of mercy are alike treated as the manifestation of the presence of the new age. . . . The all-inclusive word, corresponding to the new reality of the Spirit's presence is the word *witness*. Within that total reality, both evangelism and service, both word and action have their place.[10]

A young Roman Catholic priest in the workers' movement in Quebec, sensitive to this integrity of the whole gospel, has written: "I cannot see myself as announcing to young workers that all men are 'adopted sons' of God, equal in dignity, if I am not already engaged in the building of a society where the dignity of each will be recognized concretely." [11]

The hungry and needy of the world are astute in sensing that the so-called messengers of God who do not express compassion may indeed be false messengers, and will therefore have nothing to do with them. Perhaps the Communists who have rejected Christ have not in fact rejected Christ so much as particular expressions of Christianity which were themselves disobedient to God's command.

Like a whole caravan of outsize camels, each loaded down with precious merchandise, the developed states lurch across the world—and there is not a needle's eye through which they can pass.

—Barbara Ward Jackson

Most of the Chinese, for instance, knew Christianity only through their bitter experience of the ruthless and humiliating aggression of the Christian nations of the West. Only a small percentage of them had had any direct contact with Christian missions, and even this was sometimes an exposure to the arrogance of an individual assured of his Western superiority. Christian missions often stood in the ambiguous position of seeking to serve, yet enjoying the protection of gunboats and the special privilege of living in China without being subject to Chinese law. To China as a whole, Christianity was associated with gunboat diplomacy and unequal treaties; foreign control of customs, post office, railway zones and cities; cruel exploitation of child labor; destruction of precious works of art; and great licentious cities like Shanghai and Hong Kong where drugs and prostitution and every form of vice flourished. How could the Chinese distinguish the kindly ministries of the missionary movement from the brutal pressures of the nations from which the missionaries came? Little wonder the Chinese Communists rejected the God of these "Christian" nations.

Development: a major task of Christian mission

It is a fact of history that development has always been one of the major tasks of Christian mission. An article on mission and development in the *International Review of Mission* of October 1969 says:

> The mission of the early Church in the Mediterranean and especially of the monks in Europe laid the foundations of a more widely based economic and social life. . . . The mission of the past 200 years to Latin America, Asia, Africa and the South Pacific has carried on this tradition. The churches of the West have raised and spent vast sums of money by voluntary offerings for the well-being of peoples far away. The churches have in fact been the pioneers in the development of peoples.
>
> The preaching of the Good News has given peoples a new sense of their dignity and rights as human beings and has stimulated the revolutionary movement toward independence. Education has helped to give peoples a new mastery over the forces of nature and to form most of the leaders who have taken their people into national liberation. Hospitals, medical care and agricultural and social work have broken down the power of disease

and alleviated some hunger and have contributed to the population explosion in those countries.[12]

Journeys to Asia and Africa reveal again and again the tremendous leadership Christian missions—both Protestant and Roman Catholic—are giving in relief, rehabilitation and development programs.

In the Bangladesh tragedy, the churches spearheaded programs to care for the hungry and to reestablish returning refugees in their homes, on their farms and in their trades. They also gave leadership in calling on governments to give high priority to rebuilding the Bangladesh economy so that the people there might look after their own needs.

In India the Christian Medical Association has launched a farsighted health care program involving Christian hospitals and government medical services. It has developed programs involving public health, population control and village health services related to the specialized hospital care available only in the larger centers.

In the hard realities of the developing country of Zambia, President Kenneth Kaunda, son of a Presbyterian minister, has established a concept of development called "Zambian humanism." In practice it involves building schools and hospitals, expanding agricultural production, struggling for justice and freedom. And all these activities are undertaken because he believes that his people are God's people, and that this is the way to make Christ come alive in his country. Kaunda explains the goal of Zambian humanism in the following terms: "Humanism can only be properly expressed through tolerance and consideration toward other human beings; freedom of expression; respect for the essential dignity and worth of the human individual, with equal opportunity for each to develop freely to his fullest capacity in a cooperative community." [13]

It is when the church engages in compassionate human service that the world begins to heed the church. During the Nigeria/Biafra tragedy many otherwise cynical newsmen and radio and TV commentators in Canada recognized the church's leadership in relief and said, "Surely this is the church's finest hour." While regular church news was hidden in the back pages of Saturday papers, the news of the church's relief activities got frequent front page and editorial coverage. An editorial in a major Canadian daily included these words:

> A small group of church leaders . . . have gone ahead on their own and made an impressive contribution to saving lives in the Nigerian-Biafran tragedy. . . . In doing so, they put the lie to the careless generalization that churchmen are exclusively concerned with their own institutions, not human welfare. In this instance, their enterprise is all that has saved this nation from moral bankruptcy in response to a distant people's agony.[14]

Development is a search for a quality of life

A major Asian conference has defined development:

> We understand development as a liberating process which enables persons and communities to realise their full human potential as purposed by God. Wherever human life is oppressed, enslaved and dehumanized there is under-development. We cannot, from this perspective, speak of "developed" and "developing" nations, . . . though the specific nature of under-development varies from country to country.
>
> Even in the economically poor countries . . . people are crying not for food alone; they need and demand freedom, dignity, justice and participation as well. Their quest is for "integral human development."[15]

C. I. Itty of India, a staff member of the World Council of Churches, has said that development is not just a matter of more food and better clothing, shelter and education. Development is fundamentally "a search for a quality of life." Both "developed" and "underdeveloped" countries are involved in that search.

To be involved in the development concern is, essentially, to be involved in the struggle of our generation to know what it means to be human, what it means to be free human beings as created by God for his particular purpose. So this struggle is a universal struggle, and we are all in the process of undermining or growing out of the underdevelopment with which we are faced.

We are also after what I would call self-reliance. We want our people to learn by themselves, with dignity and freedom, to work out a little more of the conditions that they could have, and thereby experience what it means to be a free human being with a self-reliant attitude. When we speak about the unity of mankind, it has to be understood as a unity born out of a free human relationship of equality—and that is one of the goals of development.[16]

Either we feed the least of these little ones or we are damned.

—Barbara Ward Jackson

Discussion of the issues of human justice and the self-development of people forces Christians to recognize that they have a definite role to play: to energize government and business to deal with these issues. The churches must therefore first become sensitized and informed themselves and then set out to sensitize and inform the decision makers.

Many people, faced by this awesome challenge, are tempted to give up before they even start because the problems seem so insurmountable and their own resources so meager. The more involved they get the more complex the issues appear and the more the frustrations grow. It is easy to become tired of trying to help.

But here we are reminded of the words of St. Paul to the congregation in Corinth: "Seeing then that we have been entrusted with this commission . . . we never lose heart." Unless the men and women in government and business are energized to hope and to action, there is little likelihood in the decade ahead that much will be done to ease the dangerous tensions building up around the world.

Six ways the church can work toward development

Partnership or Privilege?, SODEPAX's 1970 report, lists six ways in which the churches can make specific contribution to the process of development in the Third World.

One . . . "to continue to *work at a concept of development that does justice to the Christian concept of man.* Implicit in the strategy we are here recommending is the perception of the level of living that men require to be fully human. Theologians and Christian social scientists need to join with experts from a wide variety of fields to establish what forms of economic, social and political values and organization are necessary to set all men free enough to establish and enjoy their own identity.

Two . . . "the churches must mobilize all the means at their disposal to *inform their own people and all men everywhere of the present facts.* . . . This is not to appeal to emotion. It is to face men with the realities of what will happen to culture, human dignity and community if we continue on the present course and what can happen if we make radical changes in the present directions. It is to ask them to consider the realism of allegedly realistic policies and structures. And it is to ask them to conceive of a more just society.

"This task of education cannot be limited to the educated westerner. It must be carried to the campesino and the kraal; to the barrio and the duka. For if partnership is more than a hollow phrase, it implies the right of all men to be informed of the facts, and to make their own judgments on them. It is no idle boast to say that the churches are the unique institution that has this possibility. It is this which makes their obligation so onerous.

Three . . . "the churches must continue to *seek and set forth a set of values which inform the judgments men make on the facts they see.* As we have already suggested, an essential component of this set of values will be love which encompasses both compassion and justice. These must be allied to a renewing vision of the unity of God's creation and the universality of Christ's redemption. Only thus can we transcend the confines of our own individual, national and racial egotism.

Four . . . "the churches must be ready to *use their powers of political advocacy* to speed not only the changes advocated in the United Nations strategy, but also the more far-ranging adjustments to the distribution of political power in the world which are implicit in the strategy which we have here outlined.

Five . . . "the churches need critically to *reexamine the use of their own funds and resources.* The churches' prophetic role demands prophetic action. For to prophesy on the greatest moral question of the day without radically reappraising their own priorities is to sabotage prophecy by hypocrisy. In recent years many churches have shown their concern by directing increasing proportions of their resources to the ends of development. But we must ask the churches to ask themselves whether the scale of this redirection is prophetic—or hypocritical.

Six . . . "the strategy we have outlined will threaten and therefore frighten many people. It may also make them feel guilty. Immediately this is a pastoral problem from which the churches cannot shrink. It is given a greater dimension by the fact that those who are fearful and/or guilty will be the powerful in both the rich countries and in the poor. It is they who will be tempted to react with violence and destructiveness. The churches, therefore, have a creative role of *helping such people adjust to the changes that are inevitable*. The church will only be loyal to herself if she remains sufficiently flexible in her ministry to help all those who suffer—even when they are yesterday's exploiters." [17]

Christian action now

Once again we must return to essentials and make our faith known by Christian action to meet contemporary needs. In the name of Christ, and in the wisdom and the power of God, let us act now to bring peace to the strife-torn places of the world, to feed the hungry, to do away with poverty, to provide guidance for the young, to speak for the underprivileged, and to show the way to those who are lost and long for meaning.

By many signs and wonders, the power of our Lord was made known in centuries past. His signs and wonders are ready today for those who will make them flesh and blood. Let us show forth the living Christ in all his power and compassion by action now.

7

life-styles of the congregation in mission

". . . a people claimed by God for his own,
to proclaim the triumphs of him who has called
you out of darkness into his marvellous light."
—1 Peter 2:9

The vision

The New Testament concept of the church is full of joy and excitement and unbounded expectation of what God can do. In the passage above, where Peter addresses the Christians as "a people claimed by God for his own," he also calls them "a chosen race, a royal priesthood, a dedicated nation."

The apostle Paul was never able to find words big enough to contain the riches of Christ and the privilege of those called to declare them. "To me, who am less than the least of all God's people, he has granted of his grace the privilege of proclaiming to the Gentiles the good news of the unfathomable riches of Christ . . . that now, through the church, the wisdom of God in all its varied forms might be made known" (Ephesians 3:8, 10). His adjectives stumble over one another in the letters to the Ephesians and Colossians as he tries to express the magnificent vitality we have freely received through the grace of our Lord. "Every spiritual blessing . . . the richness of God's free grace . . . the wealth and glory of the share he offers you . . . how vast the resources of his power open to us who trust in him . . . far above all government and authority, all power and dominion, and any title of sovereignty that can be named." He sees the Christ as "the image of the invisible God; his is the primacy over all created things. In him everything in heaven and on earth was created, not only things visible but also the invisible orders" (Taken from Ephesians 1).

And then he relates this One who is the power in all creation to the church: "He is, moreover, the head of the body, the church. . . . For in him the complete being of God, by God's own choice, came to dwell. Through him God chose to reconcile the whole universe to himself, making peace through the shedding of his blood upon the cross" (Colossians 1:18–20).

The actuality

What a contrast between this magnificent concept of Christ and his church and the actual image projected by the average congregation. Instead of explosive excitement at being the people through whom God's purpose of saving all creation will be accomplished, one finds a rugged sense of duty and a mild satisfaction in small accomplishments. The image many congregations have of themselves is decidedly non-missional, and the spirit of their congregational life lacks the deep excitement of those who have discovered the pearl of great price.

The great European theologian Karl Barth, commenting on the pronounced lack of joy in the church, explains it in terms of the general unreadiness of the church for mission. He observes there is a yawning gap between the church and the world. Often it is not at all apparent that the church exists for the world, and not for itself. When the church lets itself become an institution of salvation only for those who already belong to it, it becomes a blind alley for the work of the Christ. And for this reason, Barth explains, it loses its excitement and joy.[1]

In a symposium on church and world published in Canada a few years ago, Michael Barkway, publisher of *The Financial Times of Canada,* wrote:

I think we are all so absorbed in trying to make our local congregation into a successful business that . . . nobody can imagine in what way we can possibly influence the great affairs of the world or bring the spirit of God into them. . . . The claims of the needy world beyond our well-heeled North America will get less than one-tenth of what is spent merely to operate the local congregations. . . . The big business [the church] clearly is not involved in trying to promote the Kingdom of God, but in maintaining and improving the comforts and conveniences and prestige of our local temples, kitchens and gymnasia.[2]

No feeling of urgency in mission

The nonmissional image the local congregation has of itself is illustrated by the comparative ease with which it can raise substantial funds for local comforts such as a bigger organ, new carpets or pew cushions, and the difficulty with which it can raise even modest sums for mission outreach.

The nonmissional self-understanding of the individual Christian is apparent in the fact that not many see their day-to-day work as being a part of God's saving activity for mankind. Too few when choosing their work ask the basic question: How can I best use the skills and resources God has given me in his saving purposes for all mankind?

In preparation for a consultation on world mission sponsored by the Presbyterian Church in Canada in 1971, studies were made by congregations and church courts across the country. A review of some forty detailed reports was most revealing.[3] It became clear that many professing Christians are not fired by any feeling of urgency in mission. There was little evidence that mission was seen as a dimension of the whole Bible, as inherent in the nature of God and his purposes, as a necessary part of our response to Jesus Christ as Lord, as the Christian's response to a world in need of redemption, or as indeed the basic purpose for which the church exists.

When the church lets itself become an institution of salvation only for those who already belong to it, it becomes a blind alley.

—Karl Barth

One presbytery reported that it felt the crisis of belief is the most important factor in the lack of concern for missions. But there was not much evidence that congregations would agree with this or would recognize lack of mission concern as a direct consequence of the content of the normal preaching and teaching they received.

Many felt that one of the basic causes for apathy in relation to world mission is uncertainty about what the church is called to do—and particularly its role in non-Christian lands. Most seem convinced that while it is worthwhile assisting in humanitarian medical and educational work in Africa and Asia, it is questionable whether we have any duty or right to evangelize people who seem perfectly happy with their own religions.

Few relate mission to the worship life of the congregation or understand that every part of the liturgy should be a declaration of some element of God's mission.

Missions are usually regarded as a program of the church, promoted by a special interest group or board of the general assembly. And so most suggestions for increasing interest and involvement in mission consisted of ways of better promotion, rather than a deeper grappling with the faith and its daily implication for church members.

Many congregations define mission in terms of attending church services and "churchy activities." They seem to spend more time discussing ways of getting people interested in church programs than they do in equipping the saints for witness or tackling problems of injustice and human need.

Who of us has not wondered to what congregation we should take a person of another faith or no faith who would like to know something about Christianity? Our congregational routines are so stylized in the modes of a former time that they do not communicate to the person from outside, or even to the serious Christian of the younger generation. It is difficult for the new Christian to learn and appreciate old hymns, to learn the language of the pulpit, to share in conservative (or radical) political opinions, to be part of a group in which there is no discussion—even to dress in Sunday best. The common forms and structures of the church often stand in the way of the gospel reaching the outsider.

This failure in mission often happens not because congregations fail in reaching their goal but because they succeed. They may have a mission goal in their minds, but the built-in goal of accepted structures is local institutional success—not faithfulness in God's saving mission.

Most congregations are essentially built on what has been called a "come" structure. The churches are set in residential communities as places to which people are expected to come. This pattern reflects the stable society of past centuries, when the aim was to provide a church in every town so everyone could come. No provision is made for a "go" structure.

My wife and I were once invited to a wedding party held in an old Presbyterian church bought by a Jewish friend for use as an antique shop above and a coffee house below. After mixing with the guests we went downstairs for refreshments. At the small table we could barely converse because of the overwhelming sound of a rock band. We had to leave early, and as we went out into the cold February night and the door closed behind us, the deafening sound was abruptly cut off. My wife remarked, "Isn't it amazing that out here we don't hear a sound?" And I could not help responding, "This church is so well built that not a sound of what goes on inside can reach the world outside."

Yes, we have built well; but the Good News is not reaching the outside world. Have we designed our buildings and formulated our liturgy, government, action and responsibility primarily for the institution itself, rather than for the world it is sent to serve? If this is a fact, we stand in danger of imminent judgment.

Life-styles to serve the incredible Christ

What then are the life-styles appropriate for those called to be part of God's plan of salvation for all the world? How can the ordinary local congregation be faithful and effective in bearing witness to this Christ and play an effective part in the cosmic partnership?

Many groups have begun to search for such life-styles, and hopeful insights are emerging. Youth groups are saying: "Jesus can't be put in stained glass anymore. He isn't dead, but alive and well, stirring things up on the streets and in the churches. He's bringing in, not the sheaves, but the revolution of human freedom and justice. He's controversial, as will be congregations that take him seriously." [4]

Jesus can't be put in stained glass anymore.

—Robert Raines

If the church does not perceive its missional nature, it will become increasingly meaningless to its members. In a stimulating paper, "Locating Our Spot in the Cosmic Partnership," Stuart Coles, a Canadian Presbyterian minister, has written:

> [The clergy] will continue to find their energies and their cunning soaked up almost one hundred percent in maintaining a religious first-aid and ambulance depot for missionaries [all church members] suffering from all sorts of chronic miseries—because they don't know that they are missionaries. They will be plagued with frustration and confusion and mystification, belligerency in the barracks for lack of a more authentic battleground, unconstructive contentions, and wholesale desertions.

Coles reminds us pointedly:

The point of a congregation is not to keep on congregating, but to keep on dispersing on its myriad missions. When it does this, then it has realistic and constantly renewed reason to recongregate—namely, to share the news. Our diet of worship must be redesigned so that explicit input comes from all the mission fields through the articulate participation of all the missionaries—that is, the whole community. The clergyman's news, biblical and sermonic, must be complemented and tested, must be given flesh and blood, by news through his colleagues in the congregation as to what is happening, here and now, to real people, in specific situations.[5]

A bold picture of the local congregation in global mission has come from the intensive studies on church renewal carried on by the Ecumenical Institute of Chicago.

Internal congregational structures and programs must always be seen in the context of the world which is the arena of the Church's mission, so that the congregational program becomes not an end in itself but a means to mission. At the same time the mission of the local church must be utterly global in its scope. In order for the local church to minister missionally to its community, it must see the entire globe as the sphere of its mission and the context out of which it renews social structures in the local setting. Anything short of this universal understanding will only maintain autonomous, uncoordinated, and parochial communities.

Specifically, the mission which is the Historical Church is three-fold:

1) to bear witness to the Word that heals the human spirit, the Word in Jesus Christ that sets men free to live creative lives;

2) to be an insistent, catalytic power within the structures of society to see that justice is imparted to all men; and

3) to stand as a sign of hope in the midst of world despair by living a style of life which speaks of the possibility of the future as we live in the present moment.[6]

Five guiding principles toward new life-styles

A Canadian-based group which studied life-styles of the congregation in mission made the following affirmations.

1. With regard to its present life-styles: the congregation must recognize its own participation in a world which continues to reject its king, and *bring its own practices and activities continually before God, in repentance and humility,* and with openness to correction and change.

2. With regard to relationship to the community: the congregation must *enquire from and listen to persons in all areas of community life*—becoming aware of hurt, injustice, and deprivation of dignity and self-reliance—and bring these concerns into their life together before the word of God, and follow God's leading in meeting the issues. The congregation must also bring the unbeliever and antagonist into its corporate life to hear and learn through them.

3. With regard to discerning God's work beyond the limits of the organized church: the members of the congregation must seek to discern God's presence in his world, confronting that which oppresses, exploits or enslaves mankind. They should *respond creatively to the cry for liberation and human development* from the Third World, and from groups in their own country and town. They should *seek to enter into this action of God along with persons of all faiths and of no faith* who are committed to that which expresses God's will and rule in human life, acknowledging that none of us is complete without his brother.

4. With regard to educating its members for decisive action in God's mission: the congregation should *pursue those forms of education which grow out of and make effective its carrying out of its mission.* Unrelated to mission, church education becomes irrelevant and hypocritical.

5. With regard to sustaining and renewing the freshness and strength of its members: the congregation should *multiply channels of the creative and redeeming love of God,* such as prayer fellowships, Bible study groups, sensitivity groups, retreats, etc., so that the healing and growth of each person may stem from and be expressed in a relationship of trust and respect.[7]

Toward new life-styles through mission action

Because our congregational life has traditionally been so inward-looking, we will need to find specific activities through which we can experience being people of God in mission.

It is proposed that special tasks of mission outreach be assigned either to existing groups, or to special ad hoc groups set up for this particular purpose. Such groups should draw together intelligent, able and concerned people, some with special competence in the field concerned, to do hard study and research together. In becoming informed, they should not only read extensively but go out and see at first-hand the problems involved.

A church—so well built that not a sound of what goes on inside can reach the world outside.

Studies should carry on to formulating precise recommendations as to what actions the congregation or individuals in the congregation might take—for the object of these studies is action as part of God's mission.

Congregations who see themselves as local units of Christ's global mission will be able to discover in their neighborhood and world many areas which cry out for Christian action. In this ecumenical era, each congregation will undoubtedly be confronted by one or more of the following situations.

1. Our communities are receiving increasing numbers of overseas students, trainees and other new arrivals. Some of these are Christian and others are firm or casual adherents of other faiths. What can we do to invite the Christians into our congregations, not only welcoming them to fellowship and worship, but also giving them opportunity to share the insights and vitality of their Christian experience? And how can we express to those of other faiths the kindly concern of Jesus Christ, and at the same time learn from them about the practices and benefits of their faiths?

2. More and more members of our congregations are now going elsewhere in the world to serve in fields such as education and industry. How can they relate effectively to God's mission in those places? And how can they establish vital relationships with Christians there? Many tourists stir up hatreds and violence by displaying their affluence in lands which have known only poverty. How can tourists make their journeys instead an occasion for Christian fellowship? What are the other problems in travel and service abroad and how can congregations prepare their members for them?

3. There are many Christians in our communities who worship Christ according to ancient traditions almost unknown to us. Most Protestants know little of Roman Catholics, and most Roman Catholics are even more ignorant about Protestants. We are all ignorant of the various branches of the Orthodox Church, yet know they form a rich part of the Christian tradition. How can we establish contact with these fellow believers, so that we may share together our

understandings of Christ, our ways of discipleship and our traditions of worship and action?

4. We now encounter at first hand people of other faiths. There are Buddhists, Hindus and Moslems in our cities and towns and smaller communities. These people are our fellow human beings, created by the same father and waiting for the same Savior. How can we become acquainted with them, inviting them to share with us their understanding of their faith, and sharing with them what we believe are the riches of faith in Christ?

5. Our world is full of racial injustice which deprives great numbers of people of ordinary human rights, or which forces them to flee their own countries as refugees. This injustice is not only white against black, but black against brown, brown against aboriginal, and cuts across many of the racial, color boundaries. What types of racial discrimination does the congregation find in its community or in its nation: Indian, black, Asian? What can we do to understand and ease the deep sense of wrong they suffer?

6. In this era no one should be more uneasy than Christians about the fact that vast numbers of us live in affluence in the midst of a world of poverty and dire need. What can Christians do to understand the problems of poverty in their own neighborhood and nation? What action can they take to remedy them? Economic inequalities are even greater on the world scene, where the gap between the rich and poor nations widens year by year. How can we work to remedy this situation through our government trade and aid policies and through the United Nations, or through direct action in churches and voluntary agencies initiating and encouraging programs of development? How can we challenge companies in which we invest, concerning their policies in countries where there is poverty and racial discrimination?

At least one group should reexamine congregational life as a whole to ensure that the major proportion of time and money and congregational activity is spent not on the welfare of the congregation itself but on God's mission. This group should examine every aspect of the life of the congregation: its finances, its meetings, its order of service, its statements of faith, its most-used hymns, its pulpit themes, etc.

Such a study should give special attention to the congregation's support of world ministries in which it participates through world mission programs of the denomination. World mission support should be seen as one of the essential instruments through which it performs its work, and members should raise questions and be well-informed as to what is being done. World mission awareness should be an integral part of the normal life of every congregation.

At the same time, the congregation must recognize that its support of the world mission and development programs of its denomination is only one part of its mission responsibility. The main thrust of its mission action should be to the needs and opportunities close at hand and largely neglected.

Any solid program of mission action will drive groups back to study, to Christian fellowship, to worship together. And such action should lead to a new examination of existing congregational life-styles, and result in changes which more truly express God's mission today.

In the full dimensions of the love of Christ

We may expect renewal in the church when we begin to take seriously our obedience in mission. It is not by chance that the promise "you will receive power" is tied to the declaration "you will bear witness for me." When we are engaged in solid programs of mission action we will be driven back out of necessity to seek dynamic resources in the Bible and the sacraments, and to receive the enabling strength of the Holy Spirit. We may expect the church to find new vitality and joy when we serve faithfully in God's mission for the whole world.

The life-styles of the congregation should be marked above all by the great humbling fact that the congregation belongs to Jesus Christ. The congregation exists not in its own strength but in the strength of the Lord, not in its own merit but in the grace of the Lord, not for its own purposes but for the mission of him who sent his Son into the world that men should not perish but have life.

Our life-styles should express a deep sense of gratitude for God's grace and power, of penitence for our preoccupation with ourselves and our insensitivity to others, of openness to God's leading, and of joyous and unbounded expectation of what he can do through us. Then we may break free from the impoverished image of Christ we have fashioned for ourselves and discover again in all its glory the full dimensions of the love of Christ.

The apostle prays for us:

". . . that out of the treasures of his glory he may grant you strength and power through his Spirit in your inner being, that through faith Christ may dwell in your hearts in love. With deep roots and firm foundations, may you be strong to grasp, with all God's people, what is the breadth and length and height and depth of the love of Christ, and to know it, though it is beyond knowledge. So may you attain to fullness of being, the fullness of God himself.

"Now to him who is able to do immeasurably more than all we can ask or conceive, by the power which is at work among us, to him be glory in the church and in Christ Jesus from generation to generation evermore! Amen."

—Ephesians 3:16–20

notes

Chapter 1

1. W. B. Yeats, "The Second Coming," in *Collected Poems* (New York: Macmillan, 1924).

2. William Temple, *The Church Looks Forward* (London: Macmillan & Co. Ltd., 1944), pp. 2–3.

Chapter 2

1. Samuel Beckett, *Waiting for Godot* (New York: Grove Press, Inc., 1954), pp. 9, 52, 91, 94.

2. John Lennon and Paul McCartney, "Help!" lines 1–4.

3. *Salvation Today* (Pamphlet prepared by the WCC Commission on World Mission and Evangelism for the "Salvation Today" conference in Bangkok, January 1973), pp. 2–3.

Chapter 3

1. Frank Borman, article in *Life*, vol. 66, no. 2 (January 17, 1969), p. 28.

2. Archibald MacLeish, "A Reflection," First appeared in *The New York Times*, 1968.

3. Arnold Toynbee, "Atomic Age Morality," *The Globe and Mail* (Toronto), December 27, 1965.

4. "Epistle to Diognetus," trans. L. B. Radford, in *Documents Illustrative of the History of the Church*, B. J. Kidd, ed. (London: SPCK, 1938), vol. 1, pp. 55–56.

5. "Ecumenical Sharing of Personnel Report," from the

DICARWS/DWME Joint Committee meeting held at Cartigny, June 1970.

6. *Toronto Star,* July 10, 1972.

7. Cf. Arnold Toynbee, *The World and the West* (New York: Oxford University Press, 1953), p. 2.

8. J. E. Lesslie Newbigin, *A Faith for This One World?* (London: SCM Press Ltd., 1961), pp. 110–11.

9. R. S. Bhandare, in an address delivered to the consultation on "The World Mission Task Today" sponsored by the Board of World Mission of the Presbyterian Church in Canada, Waterloo, Ontario, June 1971; hereafter cited as "the Waterloo Consultation."

10. Statement by the Korean Christian Church in Japan, printed in *Preparatory Studies* for the Waterloo Consultation (Toronto: Board of World Mission, The Presbyterian Church in Canada, 1971), p. 2.

11. John G. Gatu, "Address to the Reformed Church in America Mission Festival," Milwaukee, Wisconsin, October 1971.

Chapter 4

1. John A. Mackay, "The Christian Mission at This Hour," in *The Ghana Assembly of the International Missionary Council,* ed. R. K. Orchard (London: Edinburgh Press, 1958), p. 104.

2. *World Religions,* prepared by the Ontario Department of Education, Senior Division, 1971, p. 5.

3. Bronson P. Clark, "Can Christians Learn from China?" in *China Notes,* vol. 9, no. 4 (New York: East Asia Department, Division of Overseas Ministries, NCC, Autumn, 1971), p. 38.

4. *Quotations from Chairman Mao Tse-tung* (Peking: Foreign Languages Press, 1966), pp. 171–72.

5. "On Talking and Listening," in *For Such a Time as This,* ed. E. H. Johnson (Toronto: Board of World Mission, The Presbyterian Church in Canada, 1971), p. 51.

6. "Christians in Dialogue with Men of Other Faiths," in

International Review of Mission, vol. 59, no. 236 (October 1970), pp. 391 & 382 (italics added); hereafter cited as "Christians in Dialogue."

7. George Khodr, "Christianity in a Pluralistic World—The Work of the Holy Spirit" (Paper delivered at the WCC Central Committee meeting in Addis Ababa, Ethiopia, January 1971), p. 4.

8. *Salvation Today* (CWME pamphlet), pp. 2–3.

9. "Christians in Dialogue," p. 387.

10. "The World Council of Churches and Dialogue with Men of Other Faiths and Ideologies (An Interim Policy Statement and Guidelines)," (received by the WCC Central Committee meeting in Addis Ababa, January 1971), p. 1; hereafter cited as "WCC Guidelines."

11. *The Documents of Vatican II* (New York: Association Press, 1966), p. 660n.

12. James Seunarine, in an address delivered to the Waterloo Consultation.

13. Donald V. Wade, "Mission and Religion/s" (Paper prepared for the Waterloo Consultation), p. 4.

14. "Christians in Dialogue," p. 387.

15. *Ibid.,* p. 384.

16. Seunarine, *op. cit.*

17. "WCC Guidelines," p. 4 (italics added).

18. "Christians in Dialogue," p. 389.

19. Donald V. Wade, in an address delivered to the Waterloo Consultation.

Chapter 5

1. Garth Legge, in an address delivered to the Waterloo Consultation.

2. Idris Hamid, *In Search of New Perspectives* (Paper prepared for the Consultation for Development, Bridgetown, Barbados, November 1971), p. 7.

3. *Ibid.,* pp. 5 & 7.

4. Roberto Padilla, "Del justo tiempo humano," trans. Claudia

Beck, in *Cuban Poetry 1959–1966* (Havana: The Book Institute, 1967), p. 529.

5. Antonio Fragoso, Speech in Belo-Horizonte, January 22, 1968, quoted in Alain Gheerbrant, *L'Église Rebelle d'Amérique Latine* (Paris: Éditions du Seuil, 1969), p. 156.

6. Douglas Webster, *For Us Men and for Our Salvation,* Church Missionary Society Annual Sermon 1972 (London: CMS, 1972), pp. 6–7.

7. Newbigin, *A Faith for This One World?,* pp. 89–90.

8. Statement of the 184th General Assembly of the United Presbyterian Church, U.S.A., quoted by Cornish Rogers, "Presbyterian Shell Game," in *The Christian Century,* vol. 89, no. 23 (June 7, 1972), p. 650.

9. Legge, *op. cit.*

10. *The Ethiopian Herald* (Addis Ababa), February 29, 1972.

11. Quoted in a Toronto paper, 1972.

12. Dom Helder Câmara, in an interview in *ISAL Abstracts,* vol. 3, no. 29; reprinted in *World Update* (January 1972), p. 1.

13. Fergus Kerr, "The Church as Social Criticism," in *Frontier,* vol. 4, no. 11 (Winter 1968–69), p. 298.

14. Robert Raines, "The New-Time Religion," in *Ladies' Home Journal,* vol. 86, no. 12 (December 1969), p. 131.

15. Wayne Clymer, in an address delivered to the Quadrennial General Conference of The United Methodist Church, Atlanta, April 1972; quoted by Cornish Rogers, "The Methodists at Atlanta," in *The Christian Century,* vol. 89, no. 20 (May 17, 1972), p. 568.

16. Haimdat Sawh, in an address delivered to the Waterloo Consultation.

Chapter 6

1. E. Lovelace, *While Gods are Falling* (London: Collins Publishers, 1965), p. 151.

2. Idris Hamid, *In Search of New Perspectives,* p. 5.

3. Dom Helder Câmara, "Development Projects and Concern

for Structural Changes," in *Fetters of Injustice,* ed. Pamela H. Gruber (Geneva: WCC, 1970), pp. 61–62.

4. Frantz Fanon, *The Wretched of the Earth,* trans. Constance Farrington (New York: Grove Press, Inc., 1968), p. 76.

5. Barbara Ward Jackson, Introduction to *World Development: Challenge to the Churches* (report of the SODEPAX Conference, Beirut, Lebanon, April 1968), ed. Denys Munby (Washington: Corpus Books, 1969), xii.

6. Gloria Maxson, "Warlords," in *The Christian Century,* vol. 89, no. 7 (February 16, 1972), p. 190.

7. Harold Sitahal, in an address delivered to the Waterloo Consultation.

8. Fanon, *The Wretched of the Earth,* pp. 77, 78.

9. *The Challenge of Development* (report of the Montreal Conference of SODEPAX, May 1969) (Geneva: SODEPAX, 1969), p. 25.

10. Newbigin, *A Faith for This One World?,* pp. 91–92, 100.

11. *Le Devoir* (Montreal), July 2, 1971.

12. Editorial in *International Review of Mission,* vol. 58, no. 232 (October 1969), p. 374.

13. Kenneth Kaunda, in an interview quoted by Creighton Lacy, " 'Christian' Humanism in Zambia," in *The Christian Century,* vol. 89, no. 7 (February 16, 1972), p. 191.

14. *Toronto Star,* February 21, 1969.

15. *Liberation, Justice, Development* (Report of the Asian Ecumenical Conference for Development, Tokyo, July 1970), p. 1.

16. C. I. Itty, in an address delivered to the Waterloo Consultation.

17. *Partnership or Privilege?* (SODEPAX and the Pontifical Commission on Justice and Peace, 1970), pp. 12–13 (italics added).

Chapter 7

1. Cf. Karl Barth, *Church Dogmatics,* trans. G. W. Bromiley (Edinburgh: T. & T. Clark, 1962), vol. IV, 3, ii, pp. 766–67.

2. Michael Barkway, "Is the Church Big Business?" in *Why the Sea is Boiling Hot* (Toronto: The Ryerson Press, 1965), pp. 9–10.

3. Cf. *Preparatory Studies* for the Waterloo Consultation, pp. 12–20.

4. Robert Raines, "The New-Time Religion," p. 131.

5. Stuart Coles, "Locating Our Spot in the Cosmic Partnership," mimeographed (1971), pp. 6, 7 & 9.

6. Prologue to *A Comprehensive Experiment in the Reconstruction of the Local Church* (Ecumenical Institute of Chicago, n.d.), p. 2.

7. Adapted from "Mission and Congregational Lifestyles," in *For Such a Time as This,* pp. 54–55.